A Passage Through
INDIA

A Passage Through
INDIA

Photographs   **Text**

Ganesh Saili   **Kamal Gill**

Foreword

Ruskin Bond

Lustre Press
Delhi ◇ Banaras ◇ Agra ◇ Jaipur ◇ The Netherlands

ISBN: 81-7436-114-6

© **Lustre Press Pvt. Ltd., 1992**

Sixth impression 2002
M-75, Greater Kailash-II Market, New Delhi-110 048, INDIA
Phones: (011) 6442271, 6462782, 6460886, Fax: (011) 6467185
E-mail: roli@vsnl.com Website: rolibooks.com

Text by Kamal Gill (© Lustre Press)

Photocredits
Ganesh Saili (© Roli Books)
Back cover, Chapter mnemonics, Pages 8, 15, 16-17, 18,
19, 20, 21, 25, 32-33, 35, 38, 39, 40-41, 49, 50-51, 52, 54, 70, 72,
73, 74-75, 79, 80, 82, 83, 90, 91, 92-93, 95, 96-97, 101, 102,
104-105, 107, 108 (top and bottom), 110, 111, 113, 115, 119,
122-123, 124, (top), 127, 129, 130-131, 136

Pramod Kapoor
Cover, Pages 6, 45, 48, 60 (top and bottom),
61, 62, 66-67, 68-69, 71, 87, 94, 133, 135

Sanjeev Saith
Pages 10, 37, 43

Taj Mohammad
Pages 46, 64-65

D.N. Dube
Pages 11, 14, 24 (right), 57 (top and bottom),
121, 124 (bottom), 126

Raghu Rai
Pages 53, 63

Ravi Pasricha
Page 58-59

Nitin Rai
Page 56

J.L. Nou
Pages 22-23, 24 (left)

Rupinder Khullar
Page 120

Gurmeet Thukral
Pages 116-117

Aditya Arya
Pages 99, 100

P.N. Ahuja
Page 112

Rohit Chawla
Page 30

Rahul Sharma (R. Fotomedia)
Pages 26-27, 29

Aditya Patankar
Pages 76-77, 84-85, 86, 88-89

Karoki Lewis
Title page

First published in 1992
Printed and bound by Star Standard Industries (Pte) Ltd., Singapore

Contents

Cover: *The harsher the climate, the brighter the colours—a gaily clad Rajasthani woman.*

Title page: *Frozen against the sand dunes, a camel covers vast distances in the desert without flagging. This animal is the mainstay of domestic and economic life in Rajasthan.*

Chapter mnemonics: *Porcelain plaques of the erstwhile state railways photographed at Baroda House in New Delhi.*

Acknowledgements

'Being at the right place at the right time' is a cliche that I have little choice but to rub in, once again. That's the only way I can explain this, my first book of pictures. Raymond Steiner, an amiable drifter through Mussoorie in the flower-age, taught me how to handle a camera. Along the road, my dear friend Ruskin Bond published my first photograph in a magazine he then edited, and we have since worked together on several projects through hilarious misadventures in the Garhwals. I am grateful to Bhawan Singh for his generous encouragement, to Prof. Sudhakar Misra for always turning up in emergencies and to Maya and Victor Banerjee for taking me on their film-crew during the making of *Where No Journeys End* and my wife, Abha for tolerance of slides everywhere, including the kitchen table.

To my parents, Mukand Ram and Savitri, and my sister Meera who went away without saying good-bye.

– Ganesh Saili

Foreword

"From New Delhi to Darjeeling, I have done my share of healing," sang Peter Sellers while tentatively placing his stethoscope against Sophia Loren's awesome ramparts. And from Delhi to Darjeeling, Calcutta to Goa, and Kangra to Kanyakumari, Ganesh Saili has followed his own avocation capturing the beauties of the Indian landscape and its people with growing skill and confidence.

A lecturer in English and American Literature at Mussoorie's post-graduate college, Ganesh first become a camera enthusiast in the early 1980s. His main influence then was the American (later Australian) Raymond Steiner, a creative and inventive photographer, who used his camera as an artist uses a paint-brush. Some of Ganesh's early efforts appeared in the magazine *Imprint*, which I was editing at the time, and later he worked with me on a number of features for other magazines, and we travelled together in the Garhwal Himalayas, gathering material for a book.

It was always fun travelling and working with Ganesh, but I must warn the reader that while it may be a pleasure to work with one photographer, it is unwise to travel with two. On one occasion we were joined by another camera enthusiast and the conversation all the way from Mussoorie to Gangotri (two days on the road) centred round 'F-stops' and 'shutter-speeds', with the result that a number of beautiful women passed by unnoticed – except by me. Naturally I was the ultimate beneficiary, but, for their own sakes, I don't think two (or more) photographers should travel together; they miss out on the scenery.

Once when footloose in Agra, we visited the Taj at high noon. The sun struck the white marble, and there was a great dazzle of reflected light. We stood there with averted eyes, looking at everything – the formal gardens, the surrounding walls of red sandstone, the winding river – everything except the monument we had come to see.

It is there, of course, very solid and real, perfectly preserved, with every jade, jasper or lapis lazuli playing its part in the overall design; and after a while we could shade our eyes and take in a vision of shimmering white marble. The light rises in waves from the paving-stones, and the squares of black and white marble create an effect of running water. Inside the chamber it is cool and dark but rather musty, and we wasted no time in hurrying out again into the sunlight.

I walk the length of a gallery and turn with some relief to the river scene. The sluggish Yamuna winds past Agra on its way to union with the Ganga. I know the Yamuna well. I know it where it emerges from the foothills near Kalsi, cold and blue from the melting snows; I know it as it winds through fields of wheat and sugar-cane and mustard, across the flat plains of Uttar Pradesh, sometimes placid, sometimes in flood. I know the river at Delhi, where its muddy banks are a patchwork of clothes spread out by the hundreds of washermen who serve the city. And I know it at Mathura, where it is alive with huge turtles: Mathura, sacred city, whose beginnings are lost in antiquity.

And then the river winds its way to Agra, to this spot by the Taj, where parrots flash in the sunshine, kingfishers swoop low over the water and a proud peacock struts across the lawns surrounding the monument.

A cloud – a very small cloud – passes across the face of the sun; and in the softened light we too were able to look at the Taj without screwing up our eyes. Its effect on the traveller is the same today as it was three hundred years ago when Bernier wrote: "Nothing offends the eye . . . No part can be found that is not skilfully wrought, or that has not its peculiar beauty."

And so, for a few moments, this poem in marble is on view to two unimportant people.

We say nothing: there is really nothing to be said.

Above: *Sunrise on Srinagar's Dal Lake highlights its tranquillity as a boat drifts gently over its waters.*

Opposite page: *The Ganga is considered India's holiest river, collective symbol of the faith of the country in its ancient legends and epics. Worshipped as a mother-goddess, and a lifeline to the sun-baked plains of the nation, it has been found that the river-waters contain little or no impurities, reflecting the popular view that its waters are untainted.*

Page 6: *Rajasthani tribals dress in riotous colours – bright pinks, reds and yellows – in vivid contrast to their bleached desert homeland. This village belle also wears some traditional jewellery (note the silver 'tikra' on her forehead) to attend the annual cattle fair at Nagaur.*

Page 8: *A Sikh youth takes a ritual wash in the holy tank that fronts the Golden Temple in Amritsar. The Sikhs are a martial community that was founded by Guru Nanak in the late-15th century and nurtured under the teachings of ten spiritual leaders called 'gurus'. The Golden Temple, also known as Harmandir Sahib, is considered their holiest shrine and is four hundred years old. Its domes were covered in gold leaf in the early 19th century by the Sikh ruler, Maharaja Ranjit Singh.*

It was, of course, different when Ganesh joined Victor and Maya Banerjee as a still photographer for their documentary venture, *Where No Journeys End*, which they made for the Indian Railways and he came back with many fine pictures, some of which appear in this book, admirably supported by Kamal Gill's informative and entertaining text.

Unfortunately I was not a part of this odyssey. Or maybe I was fortunate, when I think of one of the film-crew who collapsed and died of altitude sickness in Ladakh.

I am glad he came back with pictures of one of my favourite train journeys – the Kangra Valley Railway. This particular journey reveals to the traveller a land of great enchantment, and is proof that the railway engineer can create a work that is in complete harmony with his surroundings. The graceful curves of the rails, the neatness of the culverts, the symmetrical design of the bridges, the directness of the cuttings – all help to throw into bold relief the ruggedness of the terrain through which this line plays hide and seek. By contrast, the journey to Shimla through over a hundred tunnels is more like boring one's way through a series of rabbit warrens. The Kangra valley railway always avoids running

headlong into a hillside. Its engineer must have been a Taoist at heart, taking Nature's way instead of opposing it.

"Romance brought up the nine-fifteen," wrote Kipling and some of *Kim's* most memorable encounters take place in trains. Travelling by train is probably the best way of seeing India and its travelling millions. Indians love to travel. South Indians make their way to the great pilgrim centres of the north, while north Indians travel to the beautiful temples of the south, and Bengalis and Gujaratis travel everywhere. Railway stations are fascinating places where saffron-robed mendicants rub shoulders with back-pack tourists and garlanded VIPs, and marriage parties are constantly on the move.

India has been described as a 'melting-pot' of races and religions. But I dislike the word melting-pot. India is *not* a melting-pot. Races and religions, languages and cultures, have very strong identities here, and they just won't melt into each other! A better word would be 'mosaic'. Yes, India is a glittering mosaic of people of different faiths and cultures, of varying climatic zones, of greenery and desert, river and mountain, wealth and poverty,

sophisticated city life and unchanged tribal living.

It is only by living or travelling extensively in India that one can pull these myriad pieces together and realise that the mosaic is indeed a beautiful one.

The pictures in this book attempt to show us something of this mosaic. Some pieces will remain elusive. But then, India too, remains elusive. Hence its perennial fascination.

Ruskin Bond
16/3/91

Ruskin Bond

INDIA

Scale: 0 200 400 600 km

Srinagar
**JAMMU &
KASHMIR**
Jammu

Amritsar
PUNJAB
Shimla
HIMACHAL
Kedarnath
Badrinath
Chandigarh

HARYANA
◉ DELHI

**ARUNACHAL
PRADESH**

MEGHALAYA
SIKKIM
Darjeeling
Gangtok
Itanagar

Jaipur
Jodhpur
Agra
U. P.
Lucknow
Allahabad
Gwalior
Varanasi
Patna
RAJASTHAN
Udaipur

Guwahati
ASSAM
NAGALAND
Kohima
Shillong
MANIPUR
Imphal

GUJARAT
Ahmedabad
Lothal
Khajuraho
BIHAR

**WEST
BENGAL**
Agartala
Calcutta
MIZORAM
Aizawl
TRIPURA

Bhopal
Mandu
M. P.
Kanha

Ajanta
Ellora
Nagpur
ORISSA
Bhubaneswar
Konarak
Puri

Bombay
Pune
MAHARASHTRA
Mahableshwar
ANDHRA
Hyderabad
PRADESH

*Bay of
Bengal*

GOA
Panaji
KARNATAKA

*Arabian
Sea*

Bangalore
Mysore
Madras
Pondicherry
TAMIL NADU

Kavaratti
LAKSHADWEEP
Madurai
KERALA
Trivandrum

Western Ghats
Eastern Ghats

ANDAMAN & NICOBAR IS.
Port Blair

Cape Comorin
**SRI
LANKA**

INDIAN   *OCEAN*

An Introduction to India

The Indian subcontinent is shaped like an upturned triangle, its base lying within the majestic folds of the Great Himalayan ranges and its apex plunging deep into the azure waters of the Indian Ocean. For variety, the Arabian Sea borders the western coast and the waters of the Bay of Bengal lap at the corners of its eastern shores. Nevertheless, India's remarkable coastline is exhaustive. From the lofty Himalayas to its apex at Kanyakumari, it measures 1,900 miles and with a total area of 32,87,782 sq. km, is roughly the size of Europe.

As interesting as its physical features is the entire gamut of climates the continent runs through, from the snow-bound Himalayan frontiers with sub-zero temperatures to the smothering tropical heat of the south, from the Thar desert where the sun is omnipresent to the wetlands of the east.

For purposes of travel or study, India can be divided into five separate geographical areas — first, the Himalayan belt — the highest mountain ranges in the world which sweep dramatically in a north-west/south-east direction from Jammu and Kashmir to Darjeeling and Sikkim in the east, cutting off the Tibetan plateau and China from the Indian subcontinent. We come then to the mighty Ganga river which rises in the soaring peaks of the Himalayas, drains the entire Gangetic plain — a flat fertile belt which drops only 200 metres from its northern point at Hardwar to Calcutta where it flows into the Bay of Bengal. The vast barren deserts of Rajasthan, amazingly beautiful in their starkness and swashbuckling history, are a separate area of travel concentration. The Indian heartlands, which form the inner core of the country, traverse Amritsar in the north across to its middle girth at Gwalior and Mandu and then drop into the arms of the rising Deccan plateau that moves along the entire central and southern peninsula almost to India's southernmost tip.

Running parallel to India's rich coastline are the Western Ghats and the Eastern Ghats — thick mountain ridges which lend a picturesque quality and character to the country's entire coastal belt, extending from Gujarat and Maharashtra in the west, around the Cape in the south, and onto Madras and Orissa on the eastern coast. As an interesting postscript one may as well know that one quarter of India is covered with thick jungles and forests and so it has a decidedly rich flora and fauna collection, not to mention the exotic and unexposed tribal lifestyle of the native people who reside in some of these inaccessible regions.

India is perhaps one of the oldest living civilizations in history. It flourished over five thousand years ago as a sophisticated and advanced society. In 2,500 BC there is evidence of the ruins of a great civilization along the Indus river and Lothal near Ahmedabad.

Great religions took birth and root in India, among them Hinduism, Buddhism, Jainism and Sikhism. Ancient Indian texts like the *Vedas* go as far back as 1,200 BC and are treasure-houses of philosophy, spiritual insight, knowledge and treatises on differing subjects like medicine and science.

Sanskrit, the root language of India, was an advanced and well formulated system, and the study of numbers and the decimal system, astronomy and medicine was evolved by great mathematicians and scientists of ancient India.

In fact, India is today an amalgam of its rich and diverse traditions; its original and authentic vegetarian cuisine and unusual, exotic meat and fish

preparations, its spices and thus its food; its exuberant and life-sustaining festivals and fairs and finally its adaptation to the modern technological musts of today which have spawned towering metropolises as cosmopolitan and industrialised as any western metropolis.

As with everything else, Indian history flows in a chequered manner. In 270 BC, a great Indian empire dominated by King Ashok, an enlightened ruler, ruled over all of India except for the southern reaches. By the 2nd century BC, the Maurya dynasty weakened and a series of invasions followed. By the 4th century BC, the rise of the Guptas brought in a period of immense prosperity and growth.

In the 11th century, the first real Muslim invasion shook the country. Despite a period of strife and resistance for the next two centuries, the Muslims wrested control from the Indian kings and ruled over India from Kashmir to Madurai.

In 1526, with the entrance of Babar, the Mughal conqueror, a new dynasty began which was to augment and absorb not only physical territories but the culture and temperament of the Indian people.

When the Europeans landed on Indian shores to trade, the Mughal rulers had Indianised themselves to such an extent that they were considered nationalists in comparison to the Portuguese, the Dutch, the French and the British – all of whom battled each other for the riches and wealth of a great civilization.

The British gained the upper hand amongst the European contenders and became a major force. By 1805, the British Crown ruled India. In 1857, the first stirring of Indian nationalism took birth and manifested itself in a call for independence, led by the redoubtable *'satyagrahi'* Mahatma Gandhi. Independence was won in 1947, though the country paid a terrible price for it – the partition of the country into India and Pakistan.

Today, India faces the twin challenges of overpopulation and poverty with the grace and patience that come with an ancient and philosophical civilization. Its modernisation process has been well paced and it has succeeded in bringing

14

in industrialisation without losing its cultural mores. The result is impressive, despite the magnitude of India's problems. The overwhelming impression that remains with the visitor is that it is not just the magnificence and amazing beauty of the country – it is the dignity of the people of this ancient civilization that prevails.

Indian cuisine is rich and varied; however, it is Indian 'cooking' that is great. It holds in its charmed circle extraordinary traditions that leave an indelible impression on the visitor. The procedure laid out in preparing and serving a meal is layered in tradition and gives an understanding not so much of India but of what life in India can mean. These traditions vary from the far north to the deep south, as much as the brewed green tea prepared in a *samovar* and flavoured with honey, cloves and cinnamon offered by a Kashmiri differs from the freshly roasted and ground coffee offered in Madras.

Indian dishes provide an amazing revelation, in subtle and piquant flavours, in the marvellous versatility and individual preparations of such pedestrian fare as lentils, of which there are an endless variety – green, yellow, black, pink, husked, dried, sprouted, steamed, fried, cooked. The result is a vegetarian cuisine in which India remains supreme. Simple grain and garden vegetables are imaginatively worked upon from the previous night and soaked, pounded, flavoured and baked to produce mouth watering meals that are casually delectable. From the feather light *idlis* of the south and the perfection of textures of rice dishes as they are selected – puffed, beaten, pressed, ground, stewed, boiled or baked, to the strongly aromatic and refreshing betel leaf or *paan*, the preparation of which is said to be an art, and finally the extraordinary succulence of skewered grilled lamb or *Mughlai murg* curry cooked and seasoned splendidly in spiced accompaniments.

Indian specialities are unlimited, be they a large range of seafood baked in tenderising papaya leaves or marinated *kababs* broiled over a charcoal fire – tropical India is a culinary paradise of spectacular proportions.

A single overriding passion which Indians triumphantly submit to time and again is their sense of pageantry. Despite its diverse regions, it awesome distances and its enormous economic and infrastructural problems, India rises above the humdrum and displays a great zest for living. Be it a festival, a market fair, a family gathering, a religious moment, marriage, a birth or even simple trading, Indians do not miss the opportunity to colour the moment with verve and glamour.

For the hundreds of Indians with simple earnings at their disposal, a colourful red *tikka* or a garland after a bath is enough for both man and cattle. Vivacious dances celebrate the events of the coming of spring, harvesting, the advent of the monsoon and the start of the winter. Oxen carts race with each other, wrestling bouts, dances and songs, boat races, processions where entire communities join in and religious and mythological folk stories that culminate in moments of rich and resplendent proportions.

__Opposite page:__ The Taj Mahal, a poem in marble, is a 17th-century mausoleum built by Emperor Shah Jahan in memory of his favourite wife, Empress Mumtaz Mahal. The monument took 22 years to build with marble that was brought from Makrana in Rajasthan, inlaid with floral motifs of precious and semi-precious stones.

__Above:__ The waters of the Arabian Sea skirt the western flank of the country, penetrating as high north as the state of Gujarat. Here in Dwarka, so it is believed, once lived Lord Krishna, the mythical god-king. His glittering capital is said to have been lost to the sea; more interestingly, marine scientists have found the remains of settlements in a watery grave that has lent further sanctity to India's ancient legends and increased the pilgrim traffic into Dwarka.

Preceding pages: *The gypsy women of Rajasthan call the whole country their home, travelling in family groups in carts, plying service-trades, trading in goods and livestock, and fiercely protective of their independence. In a land known for its colours, the Banjaras assail the senses with their flamboyance.*

Opposite page: *In Bengal, the cult of the Devi as the mother goddess enjoys almost fanatic popularity. If Durga is her benevolent form, as Kali she is to be dreaded. During Diwali, prayers are said before her image, and then the idols are bid farewell and immersed in the waters of the Hooghly, as the Ganga is called in Bengal. Devi prayers and farewells are major socio-religious events in the state.*

Above: *Railway stations in India are usually located in city centres for they form the major means of transportation hubs between different destinations, with the railways alone ferrying as many as eleven million people every day. This scene of the railway station at Madras is common all over the country, for it is as much a ritual for family and friends to see off passengers as to receive them.*

Trains form the lifeline of the country, connecting picturesque lands and fascinating terrain with a people who embody in them the enchantment of the country. Here, a train thunders over a bridge over the Dudhsagar falls in Goa short of the town named after the Portuguese traveller, Vasco da Gama.

Bombay's Victoria Terminus is no mere railway station; it is a prominent city centre around which metro life ebbs and flows. Built of yellow sandstone and granite, it is one of the finest examples of British Raj architecture, combining elements that are distinctly Gothic and Victorian, and embellished with blue-gray basalt that has been sculptured in fine detail. The handsome building could have been anything but a railway station, and in fact, in recent times, was converted into a public art gallery in a unique experiment of taking contemporary art to the people.

Preceding pages: *The major festival of Orissa is the Rath Yatra, loosely translated as the Car Festival. Usually held in the monsoon month of July in the seaside town of Puri on the Bay of Bengal, it recreates the journey of Jagannath, the Lord of the Universe, from his temple abode to his summer palace and back. Throngs attend the ritual, annual journey, giving rise to the word 'juggernaut' in the English language.*

Above, left and right: *The faces of India tell their own tales. A young boy is dressed to play the part of Ram, the hero of the Indian epic 'Ramayan' during Dussehra festivities, while for the older, south-Indian boy, prayers are a daily feature, and the caste marks on the forehead are worn with pride.*

Opposite page: *This Garhwali bride, radiant in her beauty, bears on her shoulders, albeit lightly, the responsibility she must carry with her to her new home. The colour red is considered auspicious, and the nose ring she wears is a traditional part of her trousseau that is an inheritance of the erstwhile Tehri Garhwal kingdom.*

24

The Himalayan Belt

The Himalayan belt is a discovery of India that is at once mystical, awesome, a challenge to man's spirit, nature in the raw, in all its bounty; wild, unfettered and beautiful beyond imagination.

Ancient Aryan settlers called these mountains 'the abode of eternal snows', Himalaya. Sometimes called the roof of the world, the cradle of legendary mountain rivers or the source of India's great spiritualism, the Himalayas in geological terms are a young mountain range. They stretch 2,400 km eastwards, are 400 km wide and have an average elevation of 6,000 metres within the central axial range. Encapsulated are ice-armoured peaks that have provided an eternal challenge to climbers; spectacular crystal blue lakes; glowing orchids and rare plants, superb wildlife sanctuaries and cool, pleasant mountain retreats. Almost unbelievably, the entire range of the world's climate, flora and fauna are to be found within five vertical miles of these amazing mountains.

The Himalayan adventure begins for India from the beautiful Kashmir vale and Ladakh in the north, and swings in a wide, deep arch to cover Chamba, Kangra, Shimla, the pilgrim spots of Gangotri, Yamunotri, Kedarnath and Badrinath, Almora and Corbett, the mountain peaks of Dhaulagiri, Mount Everest and Kanchenjunga, Darjeeling and Sikkim in the east of the Indian subcontinent. Enroute unfolds a panorama of differing cultural mores, exotic people, architectural styles, dress, religion and language. A constant, steadfast experience is the warm and considerate hospitality of the mountain people throughout the Himalayan belt.

Kashmir: Kashmir remains a byword for nature's unusual beauty. In this lush and green mountain state, autumnal colours of rust and gold vie with pink apple bossoms, saffron fields, blue lotus lakes and crisp air fragrant with pine-scent and bird-song.

Srinagar is the gateway to Kashmir, and its capital. This historic valley has been the summer retreat of Mughal emperors, British viceroys and princes, and continues to play host to the many nature lovers and international leisure travellers who come here through the year. The live-in houseboats with their striped awnings and canopied sundecks on the Dal and Nagin lakes offer a romantic holiday that is unique to this valley. Handicrafts — be they walnut carved furniture, papier mache or woven carpets, shawls or silks — are a way of life for these gifted people. Kashmiri cuisine is renowned for its succulent meats, *koftas* and lamb delicacies, and the *wazwan* feast is truly the kind of festive culinary cuisine repast gourmets dream of.

Its scenic beauty resulted in Kashmir being coveted always by the rulers of India's hot plains, but it was the Mughal *sultanate* of Delhi and Agra that gave it much of its prestige. The emperors journeyed here to summer in the valley, and nature was enhanced when they bequeathed it formal gardens, waterfalls and water channels and pleasure pavilions. The British followed, and since a local regulation forbade them the ownership of land, an officer had a houseboat ordered as his residence, the start of a maritime holiday industry with houseboats that bear such exotic names as *Paradise Queen, Pleasure Palace* and *Zeenat Mahal*. Houseboats in turn are served by a network of *shikaras*, skiffs with 'spring cushion seats' that form a major means of transport, function as floating markets (everything from flowers to groceries) and row children between home and school. Today's traveller can stay in a lakeside hotel on the Boulevard, or in a houseboat with its personalised service and exquisite fittings, tour the lakes on *shikaras*, motorboats or even

water-skiis, trek, bicycle or drive to places of sightseeing splendour, and enjoy the legendary charms of the valley that have always associated it with romance and royals.

In the higher reaches, nearer 2,370 metres, the green meadows of Gulmarg and the mountain retreat of Pahalgam provide some of the finest sport in the world – riding, golf at 3,370 metres, angling, trekking, mountain climbing and white water rafting in the Lidder river during summer, and superb ski-runs between 8,700-10,500 feet and other snow sports in the winter.

Pahalgam is also the starting point of most treks and excursions into the mountains and to the snow bound sacred shrine of Amarnath at 3,800 metres which involves some adventurous trekking between the months of July and September through pine forests, high altitude lakes and meadows, frozen glaciers and snow bridges.

Ladakh: One of nature's greatest paradoxes can be seen across the 3,500 high Zoji-La pass when one leaves behind the lush green Kashmir valley and

crosses into the strange stark beauty of Ladakh's barren landscape. Dominating the lofty desert plains and sand dunes at valley heights of 8,000 ft-15,000 ft are snow capped peaks and the world's largest glacier outside the polar region – the Siachen.

Remote, yet never isolated, it is the river Indus (known in Tibetan as *Sengge Chhu* – lion mouth which spouts water) which starts at the base of Mount Kailash and is the lifeline of Ladakh. One of its tributaries is the beautiful Zanskar river. Most habitations are located along the river courses, and it is an amazing sight to see the Bactrian two-humped camel walking alongside the yak, major means of transportation here.

An equally incredible sight are the beautiful highland lakes at 14,000 feet, such as the 150 km long and 4 km wide Pangong Tso, a stunning crystal blue against barren sand dunes and ice capped mountains.

Windswept, rocky escarpments and barren plateaus reflect the light of the sun in colours of purple, blue and red. Carved into these rocky mountains are the stark, ancient monasteries of Ladakh. Leh, the provincial capital, is the base of visits to the *gompas* of Hemis, Alchi and Spituk. These *gompas* or monasteries dominate the mountainscape and have been grandly conceived with rich wood carvings, statues and frescoes. Their silent, sombre interiors are alive with vivid *thangkha* paintings, and congregations of ochre-clad monks in silent prayer or chanting the holy verses. Their large central courtyards are the focus of colourful dance and mask dramas as part of religious festivities.

A multi-racial people, the tall and wiry Ladakhi in their woollen robes and colourful girdles are known for their tolerance, grit and hardiness. And in their arid fastness, they have put together a world of active interests, with archery, polo, riding and white water rafting on the rapids of the Zanskar and Indus rivers as forms of recreational sport.

Kangra and Chamba: Nestled at the base of the Dhauladhar range of the Himalayas is the gentle Kangra valley. Flowers carpet it, emerald turf and green meadows are fringed by thick forested hills atop which sit ancient forts and castles. It is a captivating journey to the ancient town of Kangra.

Kangra itself is an old Rajput township. It was traditionally a feudal stronghold and was strategically built overlooking the Banganga river. It has been the home of exquisite miniature paintings and several ancient temples. So rich was this city in olden days that the fearsome Mongol emperor, Timur, actually sent a troop to loot the town – which it did. Even today, the township is dotted with legends and historic settings, both romantic and moving.

Travelling further up, in dark, pine covered mountains, one arrives at the rugged hill station of Dharamsala, sitting atop a spur of the Dhauladhar range. Presently the home of the Dalai Lama – the spiritual head of the Tibetans – and the many displaced Tibetan refugees – Dharamsala has all the atmosphere of a tiny Tibetan township. The great rock wall of Dhauladhar dominates Dharamsala and lends it a character in keeping with its present stoic history.

Another quiet and almost forgotten hill retreat is Dalhousie, named after one of the British governor-generals. Skirting five hills, Dalhousie commands a fine view of the distant plains on the south and snow ranges to its north. It has always been, and still remains, a quiet retreat offering a charming hill holiday.

Dalhousie is often called the 'gateway to Chamba – the valley of milk and honey'. Once again it is the valley that is famous for its sparkling springs, its lush meadows and rich countryside. The town of Chamba, which gets its name from the scented Champa blossoms of this region, has a picturesque setting on a high flat shelf overhanging the rushing waters of the river Ravi. In an abode of gods, Chamba is even more generous. Temples abound, their distinctive stone architecture and groupings all the more unique here. And away from the temples, the legends that permeate the atmosphere translate themselves into colourful embroidery on scarves for which Chamba is particularly well known.

From Kullu to Lahaul: Adjoining Kangra is yet another, albeit smaller, lush Himalayan valley, that of Kullu. Travellers have, for long, made repeated references to the unusual beauty of this narrow 80 km strip on either side of the Beas river. The Kullu valley begins at the charming temple town of Mandi at the foot of the hills and climbs alongside the Beas gorge. Never more than a mile wide, this serene valley combines its placid beauty with the dramatic surge of steep rising mountains on either side. The hillsides are naturally rich with apricot, plums, peaches, cherries and the famous Kullu apple, orchards vying with wild blossoms, flaming yellow butter cups, giant scarlet rhododendrons and blue and purple iris.

Kullu is known for its colourful fairs, festivals and religious shrines. The annual Dussehra celebrations are a big draw, an occasion for the hill-people to

Pages 26-27: The Himalayas are the world's highest, and youngest, mountain chain, dramatically outflung against the sky. The mountains crown the country and provide a natural barrier as boundary. They stretch 2,400 km in length, are 400 km wide and have an average peak elevation of 6,000 metres.

Page 29: Buddhist celebrations in the highlands of Ladakh are often spectacularly colourful ceremonies, rich in ritual and pageant. Isolated for centuries, these have become repositories not only of faith but of a way of life.

Opposite page: The water-people of Kashmir live in doongas or large family boats which serve as their home and which are also often moored strategically to function as shops or even floating restaurants.

gather, accompanied by idols of their village gods, to pay homage before Lord Raghunath. At the top end of the valley, amidst pine woods, sparkling streams and green meadows is the splendid hill resort of Manali. Manali is the starting point of treks, hikes and, in good weather, drives to Rohtang Pass and across into the wild, barren splendour of the Lahaul and Spiti valleys.

This rugged land of rocky crags, perpendicular cliffs, ice-mountains and blue-green glaciers is the home of Mongolian descendants who practise Buddhism.

Separating the areas of Kullu from Lahaul and Spiti is the Pangi range of mountains with yet another relatively little known valley of great beauty – the Pangi valley. Not only is the Pangi region rich in wildlife and scenic splendour, its vibrant folk dances and unusually handsome women have made it the destination of many seasoned travellers.

Shimla and its environs: A startling journey of hairpin bends along a well-maintained metalled mountain road leads to the bustling former summer capital of British India and the present capital of the state of Himachal Pradesh, Shimla. Of course, for those with the leisure of time, a more fascinating journey is by toy-train from Kalka to the capital. Shimla has developed from a stately summer resort into a full blown, year-round hill metropolis. Its infectious holiday bonhomie, happy crowds and bustling activity make it a holiday resort of immense popularity. Deodar and pine forests, fruit orchards, springs and streams and flower-carpeted meadows give Shimla a rare charm.

Named after the goddess, Shamla, the hill-retreat was founded by a British soldier who also built the first British residence here. In years to come, Shimla became India's summer capital, the seat of the British government, and in time gained the rather dubious reputation of a scandal-capital. Young British girls who summered here, away from England, often unescorted, in search of husbands, and married women who undertook liaisons while their husbands did duty in distant outposts, lent colour to Shimla. So much so, in the afternoons the ladies would journey, decorated with coats of arms, to gather at Scandal Point for tea and the latest gossip.

Shimla also gained some handsome buildings, many of them still standing. These included the Gaiety Theatre on the Mall, the Viceregal Lodge that is now the centre for the Indian Institute of Advanced Studies, and Wildflower Hall, now a hotel. A little more crowded now than in those early years, Shimla does not disappoint. The views are still fantastic, the crowds still surge on the Mall, and all around are wonderful new resorts where one may explore, and perhaps stay, in an environment more relaxed, less charged, than that of Shimla's.

Continuing north are a large number of local holiday spots such as Naldera, Kufri and other Himalayan retreats. Two other unusual hill resorts in the region around Shimla need to be mentioned – the picturesque hill station of Kasauli, and the scenic remote resort of Chail, where the high spots are a beautiful palace cum hotel and one of the highest cricket pitches in the world. Chail, on a hill opposite that of Shimla, was ordered by the Maharaja of Patiala when he was banned entry into Shimla. His fault – unbecoming conduct with an English lass. He vowed to make Chail more attractive than Shimla, and its dense forests and the stately palace are certainly a retreat of some dignity.

The Garhwal Himalayas: This mountain region, though traditionally on the pilgrim's trail for every religious Hindu, has lately won recognition as one of the finest trekking regions of the world. Magnificent gorges, canyons, forests, torrential rivers, glaciers and mountain ranges have made this region the retreat of great Hindu thinkers, seekers and ascetics. Religious temples of great antiquity draw scores of pilgrims, beckoning from remote, untrammelled reaches.

Apart from the holy shrines of Kedarnath, Badrinath, Yamunotri and Gangotri, an infinite number of routes for summer and winter trekking trail through magnificent mountain territory. Amongst the most well known of these is the trek to the Valley of Flowers which is 10 km in length, 2 km in width, surrounded by the river Pushpavati and home to a thousand varieties of rare and splendid blooms of flowers, shrubs, orchids and foliage. In fact, so rare is the environment of the Valley of Flowers that entry to it is controlled and overnight camping no longer permitted.

High altitude treks include the adventurous Nanda Devi sanctuary trek where, at a height of 4,500 metres, majestic peaks, wildlife, green meadows and waterfalls outdo each other in splendour.

Winter treks which promise good skiing are the slopes of Auli and the Chamoli district, both of which are rich in flora and fauna. River running between Devprayag and Rishikesh has won international acclaim and this area is a well organised sport section for the adventure seeker.

Mussoorie and Chakrata, at the base of the mountain region, are gentle holiday spots full of wooded groves, waterfalls, picnic spots and pine forests. Mussoorie, in fact, is a throwback to the British Raj with its charming hill cottages, its many schools, and a lifestyle that is considerably more leisurely than elsewhere in the country.

Corbett country and Kumaon: At the foothills of the Kumaon Himalayas lie the famous grasslands and *sal* forests of Corbett country. It was here that tigers once walked wild in large numbers and were given international recognition in naturalist Jim Corbett's lively tales of true adventure. Today a 125 square km wildlife sanctuary encompasses the area and is abundant in its population of tiger, elephant, leopard, black bear, deer, python and river animals. In fact, it was here that India's famous conservation programme, Project Tiger, was launched, and here too that Billy Arjan Singh and his attempts at releasing a pet-tigress in the wilderness were successfully recorded.

Travelling north of Corbett, into the mountains, one comes to the beautiful lake district of the Himalayas. At 6,500 ft is the hill resort of Nainital, set picturesquely around a willow-edged lake. Water sports, particularly yachting, are a traditional favourite in this area, and gaily coloured sail boats skim across the tranquil waters around which the settlement has grown. Amongst the better known lakes in this region are Bhim Tal, Khup Tal, Naukutchia Tal and a number of lesser known diamond shaped lakes. They allow for invigorating treks and a wonderful holiday in the Himalayas.

Raniket and Almora are both excellent resorts which command panoramic views on account of their position on high ridges. Both resorts have beautiful, thick forests of pine, oak and cedar and are a base for mountain treks. The tiny little town of Kausani higher in the mountains is an ideal trek because it offers a fascinating panorama 200 km across the snow covered peaks of the Himalayan ranges – including Nanda Devi and Trishul.

From Almora, the Pindari glacier is an exciting trek. Dark green pine forests intersperse dramatic ice-mountain peaks and culminate in a fairytale garden of wild shrubs and rhododendrons.

Darjeeling and Kalimpong: As one travels to the eastern section of the Indian Himalayas, to the north of West Bengal is the 'queen' of hill resorts Darjeeling. Blessed by nature, Darjeeling and its environs are replete with rich tropical forests, terraced rice fields, flower covered slopes, two fascinating Buddhist monasteries, a charming 'toy' train with perhaps the highest railroad station in the world at 2,438 metres, a fine race course, a high

Pages 32-33: *The Ladakhi countryside consists of mostly rugged mountain terrain, nestled among which are few oases of green around which settlements have grown. The provincial capital, Leh is located in typical high-altitude desert wilderness. Once a Dogra stronghold, the crumbling 19th century palace of Zorawar Singh overlooks the valley-settlement.*

Above: *Life in Ladakh can be excruciatingly difficult, for there is but a short summer in which to work in the fields and trade; in the autumn, men and women together complete threshing activities in preparation for the ordeal of winter that will keep them indoors with their livestock.*

altitude zoo and rare orchid hot-houses and botanical gardens.

As if this were not enough, Darjeeling affords one of the most splendid sunrise views of snow-kissed mountain peaks in this part of the great Himalayan range – including Mount Everest and Kanchenjunga, which are a clear 100 miles distant.

But, more than anything else, Darjeeling is symbolised by tea plantations. The leaves of the delicate yet distinct Darjeeling brew are famous the world over. Indeed, the journey to Darjeeling is through several of these plantations, looking all the while like manicured pincushions of green baize. To actually sit in a Darjeeling hotel's garden and sip the brew is an altogether rare privilege.

The tiny resort of Kalimpong is another enchanting place with colonial villas, deep forests, rare orchids and many flowering shrubs, a colourful tribal population and a Tibetan monastery. An enterprising experiment has led to the formation of a dairy in the Swiss style that provides sweet candies and excellent cheeses. Further east is the former princely state of Cooch-Behar, famous for the rich reserve of the Jaldapara game sanctuary and a thickly forested region rich in flora and fauna.

The North Eastern Himalayas: 'The Mantle of the Rising Sun' or Arunachal, a north-eastern state, and 'Home of the Clouds' or Meghalaya, another state in the region, are named for the kind of descriptive phrases typifying the imaginative and vivacious nature of the eastern Himalayan region.

Shillong is a charming retreat in the tranquil Khasi Hills of Meghalaya. Its pine woods and gently rolling hills, its lakes, streams and waterfalls make it a favourite holiday spot. The Khasis were once a matrilineal society, and women play a major role in the state's social lifestyle. Orchids bloom here, and fruit orchards are plentiful. Cherrapunjee, close to Shillong, has the distinction of being the wettest place on earth, recording the highest year-round rainfall.

The people of Assam and their great tribal heritage, the rich reserves of thick forests, and the abundance of wildlife sanctuaries that dot the Assamese countryside give it the nomenclature of 'the last frontier'. Even today, some tribal reaches are primitive and so culturally inviolate by modern day living as to make it a great experience for the naturalist, environmentalist and adventure seeker.

North of Shillong, to Guwahati on the banks of the great Brahmaputra river and moving eastwards to the Kaziranga sanctuary, one comes across miles of tea gardens, evidence of the famous Assam tea. A great delight in this region are the sanctuaries. The Kaziranga National Park is home to the great one horned Indian rhino in its last bastion. Wild elephants and swamp deer provide exciting viewing, and the uncommon, 16-foot tall elephant grass which covers the reserve makes sightseeing on elephant-back almost mandatory. The other sanctuary, about 85 km west of Guwahati at the foot of the Bhutan hills, is Manas. Beautifully picturesque, with the sparkling river Manas flowing though the preserve, Manas is well known for its tiger population and other big game, leopard and black bear and, of course, the rhino.

Sikkim: One of the most fascinating of the north eastern states is Sikkim. This principally Buddhist region was closed in from external influences till very recently, and so a lot of the traditions have survived in their purest form. This is the land of the mythological dragon, and here this legendary reptile can be seen woven into carpets, beaten into gold jewellery, carved into wooden furniture. Monasteries abound, and in fact the Rumtek monastery is the abode of the spiritual leader, the Karmapa. Rumtek is at some distance from the state's capital, Gangtok, and the distance in between is filled with high mountains and sheer, cliff-hanging valleys through which the river Teesta flows. Here too are orchidariums and orchid sanctuaries, for Sikkim has an amazing density of flora to its credit. So incredibly rich is this natural resource that from April to May the state hosts an international flower festival.

Sikkim pays homage too to Mount Kanchenjunga, the high Himalayan peak held sacred by the people and worshipped as a god. But there are high Himalayas all around too, and in their folds are a number of monasteries, rich with the flavour of Buddhist legends. Ochre-clad monks crowd their halls in prayer and during festive periods the courtyards are a pageant of colour as locals gather to witness the mask-dances.

In recent years, Sikkim has become rather well known for its treks. Through some bewildering scenery, trails ripple along hillsides, the route often decorated with fluttering Buddhist prayer flags. Gentle people nod at strangers. This, indeed, is Shangri-la.

The north-eastern Himalayas include a number of smaller hill states, all close to the Indian border with neighbouring countries. These include Arunachal, where the forested mountains provide sanctuary to a large number of Buddhist monasteries, among

them the Tawang monastery with its very rich gold-leaf manuscripts in its library, and several remote nunneries dedicated to the faith. Mizoram is still a closed state, but in Nagaland the capital, Kohima, has some excellent sights including the British war cemetery which marks the point of advance of Japanese troops into India during the Second World War. Tripura, a smaller state, is best known for its woodcraft.

Shikaras are gondola like boats that form the major means of transportation on the Dal and Nagin lakes in the Kashmir valley. Shikaras are attached with houseboats for ferrying guests; local residents find them useful for sending children to school, or the women to the shops. The more enterprising among local residents ply them as floating, mobile shops that sell everything from tourist souvenirs – including priceless carpets – to groceries and household items.

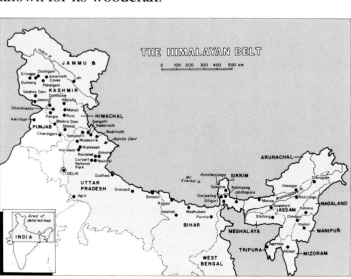

Pilgrim's Passage

In the hidden recesses of the great Himalayas lie some of India's most sacred spots. At 3,900 metres, in ice-bound magnificence, are the secret sources of India's holy rivers – the Ganga and the Yamuna.

The Ganga, which is the Hindu umbilical cord, the cradle of its great civilization and a perennial source of spiritual vitality, spouts at 'the mouth of the world' or Gaumukh. Enormous ice-sheets lend an awe and natural reverence to this pilgrim spot. The Bhagirathi, as the Ganga is called here, flows through glaciers and frozen valleys which are enclosed by towering ice walls such as Mount Shivling.

At a height of 4,138 metres, in the remote silence of snow and ice, stands the great temple of Gangotri, where the Ganga is said to have descended from the heavens. According to legend, such was the force of descent of the river goddess, her waters had to be trapped within the locks of Shiva's hair before being released on earth. However, there is a physical descent of some 900 metres from the source of the river to the temple at this point. Ascetics and hermits are the only reminders of human presence.

At Devprayag, another holy site, the Ganga has become bigger, more swift, and flowing fast over rapids and falls. Many stretches of the Ganga have today achieved international fame as ideal for river running and white water rafting.

In the ice-bound regions of the Himalayas lies the source of another holy river – the Yamuna. This spot is called Yamunotri and has an ancient temple dedicated to Goddess Yamuna. The hot springs in this sacred area are a major draw for pilgrims.

River goddesses: Holy sites along the route mark the progress of Indian rivers. One such is the scenic area of Badrinath, nestled between towering ranges and a snow-bound landscape. At this point the river Alaknanda meets with the Rishi Ganga and pilgrims celebrate the confluence with ritual prayers along the banks (marked by temples) and holy dips in the cold waters.

Four hundred metres higher than Badrinath is Kedarnath, another fascinating pilgrim spot, dedicated to Lord Shiva. One of the twelve *Jyotirlingas* of Shiva, a beautiful and ancient temple stands on a high-rise overlooking the flower-strewn Mandakini valley.

The first large pilgrim centre on the Ganga is found on practically the last curl of the river's mountain course. Rishikesh is the name of the placid pilgrim town that basks in the sun on the banks of the Ganga. Here ascetics, *sadhus* and preachers mingle with seekers and common pilgrims who visit the town. Several quiet retreats in the simple *ashrams* along the river banks give Rishikesh its particular character. The town is characterised by its cantilever bridge, Lakshman-Jhoola, which is well documented in Indian folklore.

As the Ganga settles into the lap of the plains – 20 km below Rishikesh at the holy city of Haridwar or 'Gateway to Heaven' – one comes upon India's most popular pilgrim centre. At Haridwar the Ganga manifests itself as a positive element of Hindu religion. Bathing ghats, temples, *sadhus* and shrines resound to the prayers of hundreds of bathers and the chant of *mantras* as it takes along flowers and lighted earthern lamps as offerings from its devotees.

In the great Gangetic plains, the Ganga comes into its own as a lifeline and a source of sustenance for India's thickly populated regions. Two big cities which follow the course of the Ganga are Lucknow

– the present capital and traditional centre of culture and music which also earned fame for its brocades, embroidery, silverware and ceramics – and the industrial centre of Kanpur. Lucknow has always held a special place in the history of India. Here, within the parameters of a noble social culture, an etiquette for fine living was slowly put together. Gourmet cuisine, cool fabrics, music and dance and formal mannerisms flowered till the British takeover and the destruction wrought on their settlement at Lucknow's Residency. Modern Lucknow still resides in the shadow of its past. Poetry marathons are held, *kababs* sizzle over barbecue embers on street-corners, and the city skyline is pierced by the turrets and domes of familiar Imambaras. At this juncture it is appropriate to spotlight the course of the Yamuna river some 160 miles northwest of Kanpur before it merges with the Ganga at Allahabad.

Imperial capitals: Travel back 160 miles along the Yamuna to the famous city of Agra, the setting for the Taj Mahal, the eternal and enchanting symbol of India that evokes instant images in the mind of every traveller. It is on the banks of the Yamuna waterfront that the magnificent marble tomb built by Shah Jahan stands. The Mughal emperor so loved his wife that upon her death, in childbirth, his tribute to her took the form of a mausoleum so magnificent that the world pays homage before it. Yet, one Urdu poet has lamented, so magnificent is the work that it makes a mockery of love in a poor man's world. Built of pure white marble, the mausoleum is perfectly shaped, inlaid with precious stones, and contains the tombs of the two lovers whose memory it perpetuates. Agra has been home to various Mughal emperors, and in turn is known also for Akbar's Fort and Tomb, the Pearl Mosque built by Shah Jahan, and Itmad-ud-daula, the exquisite tomb said to be a precursor of the Taj Mahal and built by Empress Nur Jahan. The handicrafts of Agra reflect its attractions, in particular marble inlay work.

Historically, the Taj Mahal took 22 years to build, and legend has it that Shah Jahan had ordered a similar mausoleum in black marble for himself on the opposite bank of the Yamuna and facing the Taj. Though work on this monument was begun, it was never completed for the 17th century emperor was imprisoned by his son who had himself crowned emperor while Shah Jahan spent his remaining years in exile, in the Red Fort at Agra.

For a monument that is so well known and so often photographed, visitors approach the 350-old mausoleum expecting to be disappointed. They never are. The Taj takes on a different hue at every time of the day. In the early morning it is a beautiful, pearly white mausoleum; in the shimmering heat of the noon-sun, it appears to float like an apparition; by moonlight, it is a concentration of man's overwhelming outpourings of romance. Over the decades, the famous and the infamous have rubbed shoulders here, and in the words of Edward Lear, the world is divided into two – those who have seen the Taj, and those who have not.

In 1783, the British painter Hodges found the Taj Mahal 'a most perfect pearl on an azure ground'; and in 1844 the discerning Col. Sleeman recorded: 'For five and twenty years of my life had I been looking forward to the sight now before me. Of no building on earth had I heard so much as this . . . and from the first sight of the dome and minarets on the distant horizon, to the last glance from my tent-ropes to the magnificent gateway that forms the entrance from our camp to the quadrangle in which they stand, I can truly say that everything surpassed my expectations'.

Yet, Agra has had to underplay its other monuments for so breathtaking is the Taj that all else pales in comparison. Agra would have been a popular city even it it did not have the Taj for it has several outstanding 17th century buildings, among them the Red Fort – as impressive as its counterpart in Delhi – the Itmad ud Daula and Sikandra. Agra was the capital of the Mughals before their final shift to Delhi, and it was here that the dazzling court that held sway over Hindustan, held *durbar*. The Taj was an embellishment to the city, and soon became its crowning glory.

THE PILGRIM'S PASSAGE

Moving northwest, one chances upon Mathura and Vrindavan – both interesting old pilgrim towns where religion and folklore connected with Lord Krishna are thriving reasons for pilgrim visits. Here the boy Krishna lived aeons ago, his mischievous childhood and his youthful dalliances chronicled in Indian mythology.

In the reverse direction, 26 miles south-west of Agra, is the amazingly preserved sandstone city of Fatehpur Sikri, deserted but imperial in its proud resistance to the onslaught of time and the foibles of whimsical emperors. Akbar, who ordered this entire city on its magnificent scale as a memorial to the seer who had predicted the birth of his heirs, abandoned it due to water scarcity scarcely 17 years after it was built.

Travelling up from Agra, 123 miles away, along the banks of the river Yamuna, is the sprawling capital of the Indian nation – Delhi. A seat of power several centuries old, Delhi commands the vital north-west approach to the fertile Ganga plain. So strategically important is this site that no fewer than eight great cities have come up in this area, each marking the beginning or end of a great epoch in Indian history.

Delhi is, thus, an intriguing city where entire remains of centuries old city-capitals mingle with the concrete and glass superstructures of a modern metropolis. Often held among the oldest living cities of the world, more than 3,000 years old, Delhi repeats its cycle of season and change – much like the waters of the Yamuna.

New Delhi, five miles south west of the old, shifts the present physical focus of the city to Edward Lutyens in 1911 and his concept of colonial India – wide avenues, huge bungalows, enormous lawns and tree-shaded boulevards. The central vista, comprising the Secretariat, Viceroy's House or Rashtrapati Bhawan, and the circular Houses of Parliament, are superb sandstone landmarks that make a sweeping historical statement of the grand empire that was once under the British Crown, and upon which, it was said, the sun would never set.

A link between old and New Delhi is a stretch of green landscaped parks and groves along the right banks of the Yamuna. Here one can stop at Rajghat, Shantivana and other memorial sites to Indian leaders.

Old Delhi is history alive. Its monuments form the nucleus of city life. Shah Jahan's Red Fort – complete with imperial palaces, spendid halls and ceilings – broods over the commerical nerve centre of Chandni Chowk – the 'moonlight square', once known as the

Pages 38 and 39: *The placid Kangra valley countryside is unchanging, a rich land where horticultural and agricultural produce is of high quality and in generous quantity. The unchanging landspace is celebrated in local art and verse, and against its timelessness, a hand-pushed trolley inspects the Kangra valley line, and cattle are used for both dairy as well as irrigational purposes.*

Pages 40-41: *The Bauls are the itinerant ministrels of Bengal who sing of the countryside, and of empires past. Interestingly, in their songs they have no distinction between the male and the female singers and therefore, the men often let their hair grow long like women. This group of Bauls was photographed outside Bolpur near Shantiniketan.*

Page 43: *Banaras, or Varanasi as it is now known, and once called Kashi, is a city that dates back to an age that identifies it among the oldest city-settlements known to man. Innumerable temples line its banks, several of which are drowned by the monsoonal swell of the Ganga. Little boys who dive off the sunken temples after tossed coins are a common sight.*

Above: *The 13th century Qutab Minar is a victory tower begun by the ruler of Delhi, Qutb ud Din in 1199. A towering symbol of Delhi, it ascends a dramatic 72.5 metres high in five tiers of fluted sandstone.*

wealthiest street in the world. The 17th century Jama Masjid resounds to the sound of the *muezzin's* call even today.

The 12th century Qutab Minar in another, earlier part of the city, is a 238 feet high sandstone tower and the 1,600 year old Iron Pillar, which stands here in the open and has still not rusted, is a marvel of ancient science. Forts and tombs form a focal point for well-laid parks. Flaming gulmohar and yellow laburnum trees are typical foliage of this green and gracious city. Old historic sites juxtapose five star hotels and ancient ruins continue to remind Delhi of its remarkable heritage.

The acceptance of Delhi as a city with a distinctive personality is difficult to make, for it wears many faces, each more bewitching than the other. The splendour of its past is always at hand, and its present has the elegant graciousness of a city that is well laid. Yet, Delhi is more than all this. It is a thieves market (Chor Bazar) on Sunday, the colour of rainbows in spring, a son et lumiere at Red Fort and the dazzle of silver and gold in boutiques. Delhi is a political capital, an administrative centre, the seat of

government. Therefore, it is also a city with considerable power-play, a city where rallies are common-place and where streets are mysteriously closed, roads blocked off, as VIPs move about in ministerial cavalcades. It is also India's cultural capital. For any artiste to make a mark, a Delhi performance is obligatory. The best painters exhibit here. And all international performances debut here. It is a city of intense activity, the pulse of India.

Holy banks: We return to the Ganga at Allahabad where due to the confluence of the rivers Yamuna and the mythical Saraswati (there is no concrete evidence of its ever having been here, but Indian mythology reflects the popular thought), the Ganga has grown to an immense size. At the 'Prayag' or confluence, pilgrims come to offer their prayers. Allahabad, however, remains more a centre of learning than a pilgrim town. This despite the fact that perhaps the largest ever festival, the Kumbha Mela, is held here every twelve years.

As the Ganga twists east and widens its girth to almost a mile, it takes on a timeless hue. It is at this point of the Ganga's growth that there appears, appropriately enough, the holiest of cities – Varanasi or Banaras. Also known as Kashi or Luminous One, the city snuggles on the left bank of the Ganga.

In its own right, Banaras is regarded as the centre of the world, the city of the gods, and is believed to be blessed with a special dispensation that ages back to the origins of creation and rebirth. There is no power greater than at Kashi and here even the god of death is held at bay. Therefore, to die in Kashi or to have one's ashes immersed here is to obtain *moksha*, or liberation of the soul.

Add to this the benediction of the Ganga and you have a profound fusion. A series of temples, shrines and bathing ghats rise in tiers, one above the other, along the river's bank. One of the most popular pilgrim circuits is to walk along the Panchkrosh road and thus 'circle the world'. Along this pilgrim route, which can take five days to cover, there are as many as 108 pilgrim shrines.

Believed to be the oldest living city in the world, with a recorded history dating back to 2,500 years, Banaras has always been a centre of pilgrimage. Crowded, noisy, intense, it reflects the true Hindu essence for this is Shiva's city of birth and death. Life is centred around the Ghats on the Ganga's banks: early morning veils of mist are lightened by the sun as it rises, unfolding a surging panorama of bathing-steps, buildings and a mass of humanity. Summon a boat, cruise down the waters, and you will be offered a wedge of the Banarasi experience – holy washes in the river, prayers to the Sun God, morning ablutions, and cremations at specified *ghats*. But for the fact that the numbers on its banks have grown, the sight has remained unchanged for centuries. Varanasi was a flourishing city even at the time of the coming of the Aryans in 900-800 BC, and references to Kashi can be found in the *Atharva Veda* (1100-900 BC).

In fact, the antiquity of the city is dated by an English historian, Sherring, thus: 'When Babylon was struggling with Nineveh for supremacy, when Tyre was planting her colonies, when Athens was growing in strength, before Rome had become known or Greece had contended with Persia, or Cyrus had added lustre to the Persian monarchy, or Nebuchadnezzar had captured Jerusalem, and the inhabitants of Judaea had been carried into captivity, she had already risen to greatness, if not to glory'. A more contemporary writer, Pramesh Ratnakar, in his treatise on Banaras, has remarked: 'In a very real sense modern Varanasi is more than a city – it is a museum palpitating with life. Time past – and it is a long past – is contained in Time present, and one can trace in its gods and goddesses, in its temples, sacred ponds and wells, in its *ghats* and festivals, in its

Above: *Many people come to Banaras for many purposes; some seek salvation, others to rid themselves of their sins with a ritual morning dip in the Ganga. Yet others come here to die, and the Kashi Mukti Labh is one place where the aged and the ill seek their peace with their creator.*

Opposite page: *Just as any other provincial city, Banaras has the immense vitality of its people to whom it is home, and who provide the city much of its character. The city-streets are aswarm with people on foot and on bicycle rickshaws, making the plying of motor vehicles in the heart of the city a job recommended only to the stout hearted.*

narrow lanes and crowds, in its pilgrims, ascetics, priests and philosphers, the very foundation of Indian civilization'.

Eight miles north of Varanasi is the Buddhist pilgrim centre of Sarnath where the Buddha preached his first 'Sermon on the Mount'. A large number of *viharas,* museums and monuments mark Sarnath.

As the Ganga traverses into the plains of Bihar, it becomes so wide that it often floods its banks. Patna is the next major city on the Ganga's long route to the sea. Close by is the town of Sonepur where the river Gandak joins the Ganga. Sonepur is a small town yet, for centuries, on the day of 'Kartik Purnima' or full moon in November, it comes alive to the faith of millions of believers who bathe at 'the domain of Lord Vishnu'.

The Ganga has several pilgrim centres along its route, the island of Jahangir being one such. Situated in the centre of the swiftly flowing Ganga, this strange island has for centuries been a hermit's retreat. A temple dedicated to Lord Shiva is visited by several hundred pilgrims. The island is replete with antique stone icons and reliefs of great artistry which bear out Hindu and Buddhist faiths.

As the Ganga moves closer to its final embrace with the ocean waters of the Bay of Bengal, a major part of its waters flow into Bangladesh.

Seeking sanctuary: A much depleted Ganga turns south and becomes renowned as the Hooghly – a shallow, broad river with the colossal power of commanding sea ports – the reason why, over centuries, its ownership has been a cause of battle by the warring kings and colonising traders who came to India. Several interesting remains of trade settlements belonging to the French, British, Danish, Portuguese and Dutch colonisers can still be found on the Hooghly. Only one of these settlements now remains – the famous harbour metropolis of Calcutta.

Offering excellent anchorage on the river front because of its deep waters, Calcutta has a mesmerising attraction. It is a city of great contrasts. It is known as much for its British heritage which lingers nostalgically in every nook and corner, as it

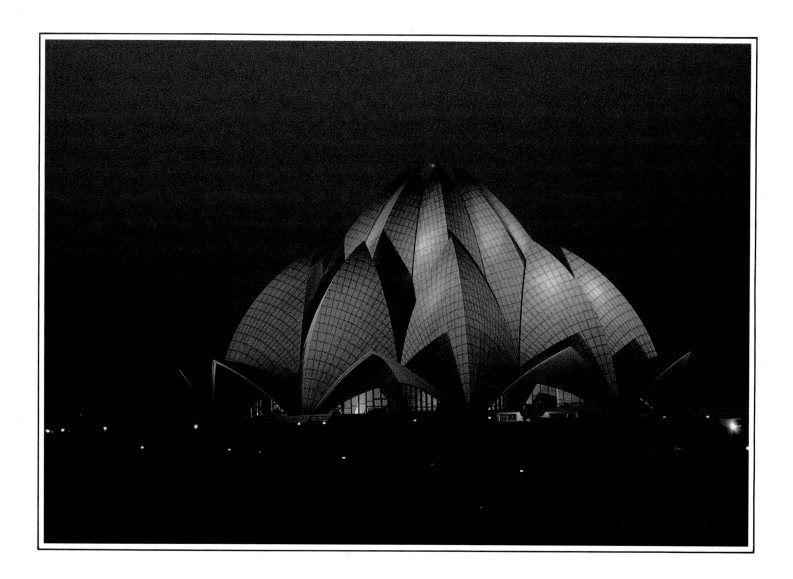

is for its artistic and traditional Bengali culture which has given birth to great philosophies, intellectual and art movements.

Calcutta, the provincial capital of West Bengal (East Bengal, under partition, became East Pakistan, and following independence, is known as Bangladesh) and the gateway to India's eastern hinterlands, only recently celebrated its tercentenary. This great city with its living vitality was founded by Sir Robert Clive of the British East India Company. Three villages on the banks of the Hooghly grew and became the entry point for British dominion in India, and the new city of Calcutta became their capital. This glittering prize housed palaces and mansions more handsome than their counterparts in Britain. And though some of the great revolutionaries came from Bengal, Calcutta still wears the symbols of her colonial heritage with grace. Her streets are crowded with Gothic, New-Colonial, Elizabethan, Regency and Indo-Saracenic mansions. The splendid Victoria Memorial still pays homage to that great queen and empress. Sports such as polo, golf, and the tradition of clubs still have a following in Calcutta. Over the years, Calcutta has

Opposite page: The Red Fort, or Lal Qila as it is known in the vernacular, is the 17th century imperial residence ordered by Shah Jahan, better known as the builder of Agra's Taj Mahal. The fortified settlement has grand public and private palaces and fronts Chandni Chowk, the 'moonlight square' that was designed by the emperor's daughter as a shopping mall and residence enclave of the rich and the powerful. In its day it was known as Shahjahanabad, the seventh known city of Delhi, as grand and glittering as the Mughal empire and its court.

Above: One of New Delhi's newest monuments is the Lotus Temple built entirely of marble, a house of faith dedicated to the city by members of the Baha'i religion. The architecture of the temple is stunning, and overlooks water pools and landscaped gardens. Within the temple, speech is not permitted and idol-worship not allowed; the visitors to the temple are expertly handled by volunteers.

become a little tattered around the edges, its aging has been dramatic and rather ungracious, yet it is a city of sensitivity and strength, alive to issues and grappling boldly with a future that holds little promise.

As if to bequeath and distribute equally its generous riches before it enters the sea, the Ganga fans out along with the river Brahmaputra into a vast delta crisscrossed with streams, waterways, riverines and creeks. Here, at this juncture, it gives birth to the largest estuary-forest in the world — an environmentalist's dream come true — the Sunderbans. In these swamps of the delta, the mangrove jungles resound to the call of abundant wildlife — rare birds, crocodiles, sea turtles, leopards and tigers.

Finally, it is at Gangasagar that the Ganga enters the sea. Even in this final stage, the Ganga waters pour with such great force into the ocean that its muddy current can be distinguished 600 km within the Bay of Bengal.

Preceding pages: Camphor flames spear the darkness that has fallen on the township of Haridwar, the temple town in the Himalayan foothills where millions come to bathe in the Ganga. The evening 'aarti' is a ritual event at the Ganga temple at Har ki Pauri.

Above: Hot air balloons take off from the lawns that flank India Gate in New Delhi on the occasion of the annual autumn Balloon Mela. India Gate stands astride Rajpath, the principal thoroughfare that fronts the imperial Rashtrapati Bhawan atop Raisina Hill. India Gate is a memorial arch dedicated to the memory of the Indian dead in the second Afghan War.

Rashtrapati Bhawan, once the residence of the British Viceroy in India, and now the official residence of the president of the Indian republic, was designed by Sir Edward Lutyens as part of the new imperial city that marked the shift of the capital from Calcutta where the British empire had struck root in India, to New Delhi. This, and the rest of the new city, sported Indo-Saracenic architecture at its grandest.

Gwalior Fort crowns this medieval settlement, dating back to the 8th century, with palaces and apartments within that have been added over the centuries. Within the fort that owes its origins to the prophesy of a saint, are some exquisitely sculptured temples, a museum with fine sculpture and ramparts that command panoramic views over the city. Gwalior has some other beautiful palaces and is conveniently connected from Delhi on the fast-link Shatabdi Express.

There is much else in Agra that delights visitors. Sikandra is the final resting place for Emperor Akbar, a mausoleum designed with bold mosaic patterns and set within a spacious garden. Begun by the emperor, the tomb was completed in 1613 by his son, Jehangir. Akbar, in his lifetime, is to be commended for giving Mughal India some of its handsomest monuments.

Above: *Though a monument of great magnificence, the Taj belongs to the soil from which it has arisen, to be enjoyed alike by royals and commoners. This is perhaps justification for the twenty-two years it took to build at the hands of twenty thousand labourers at a monumental cost that has never been precisely tabulated. In the end, the Taj was topped with a gold fillial which, however, was ransacked under the British occupation of Agra.*

Opposite page: top and bottom: *At the heart of the Taj, deep within its bowels, are the cenotaphs of Mumtaz Mahal and Shah Jahan, the emperor's more ornate than his beloved's. The marble screen surrounding them is heavy with pietra dura inlay of lapis lazuli, carnelian, jasper, turquoise, agate, coral, garnet, diamond, rockspar, lodestone, onyx, chalcedony, amethyst and sapphire. The screen alone took ten years in the making. Shah Jahan's cenotaph is topped with an ink-well.*

Pages 58-59: *The Taj Mahal is perfectly proportioned, exquisitely detailed. Still white, 340 years after it was built, it comprises a forecourt, a majestic entrance leading to a formal Mughal garden with the usual water channels and fountains, the mausoleum itself with its domed two-storied building flanked on four sides by minarets, an attached mosque, and a crypt in which the royal graves have been placed.*

Opposite page, top: *An aerial view of Fatehpur Sikri with almost the whole imperial complex in view; in the foreground are the Buland Darwaza and Salim Chishti's tomb; the tiered Panch Mahal too is visible. Fatehpur Sikri was built by Emperor Akbar as his new capital, but abandoned soon after as it suffered water shortage.*

Opposite page, bottom: *An aerial view of Agra Fort from the east. The prominent white building visible is Moti Masjid, the 'pearl mosque' which was later replicated at the Red Fort in Delhi by Emperor Aurangzeb. Shah Jahan was imprisoned here by Aurangzeb and held in captivity till his decease.*

Above: *The Yamuna has moved away a little since the three centuries and two score years when the Taj was first built. Despite that, its location has been singularly well chosen, on a bend of the river. Efforts are now being made to declare the sites around the Taj a sanctuary and ensure its pristine environment.*

Above: *Deposed by his son Aurangzeb, and imprisoned within the Agra Fort, Emperor Shah Jahan spent the rest of his life looking out along the river Yamuna to the perfect, extravagant monument he built for love of his wife Mumtaz Mahal.*

Following page: *The final resting place of an emperor and his dream: Shah Jahan's cenotaph at the Taj Mahal in Agra.*

Pages 64-65: *Mornings find the bathing ghats of Banaras crowded, for it is widely held that the Ganga in this Shiva city is holier than elsewhere, and so a dip in the river-waters here absolves one of all sins.*

Pages 66-67: *The most popular of the river ghats is Dasashwamedha, possibly on account of its easy accessibility. The ghat houses three ancient Shiva lingams and is closest to the gilded Vishwanath temple.*

Pages 68-69: *Manikarnika Ghat, considered the most sacred in Banaras, is said to be the point where Lord Shiva created the universe, and it is held that it is this spot that will survive the universal holocaust. Vishnu is said to have toiled here too in creating a pool, and his footsteps are enshrined in marble on the steps of the ghat.*

Above: *A colourful collage on the steps of a ghat in Banaras is composed of pilgrims drying their clothes after an early morning dip in the Ganga.*

Manikarnika Ghat is also where Hindus
come to cremate their dead, for to be consigned to the flames
here is to obtain freedom from the chain of rebirth. Funeral
pyres burn night and day, the holy flame nurtured by a
community called the Doms who supervise the burning of the
dead at this ghat.

*Calcutta's most enduring symbol, and a very important
communication link across the banks of the Hooghly
(another bridge is under building) is the Howrah bridge, the
largest cantilivered structure in the world and built in 1941.
The bridge has eight lanes for traffic, tram tracks and
pedestrian pathways where hawkers peddle every item of use
– from fish to toothpaste.*

Great care goes into the making of Kali and Durga images in Bengal. Preparations begin a few months before the festivities; the idols are moulded, painted and clothed with great care. Eventually, following the celebration of Kali Puja, the image will be surrendered to river-waters. Here, an artist brings distinction and detail to bear on his images near Adampur.

Desert Cities

There is a certain enchantment that the desert state of Rajasthan evokes. This is a land of bare rocks, sandy desert, limpid blue lakes, mountains and even jungle tracts; the home of the martial knights, the Rajput race whose chivalry, dare-devilry and astounding courage have produced a great history. Carved into the rocky embattlements and superb forts and palaces are stirring legends of their prowess in war and their sensitivity to aesthetic beauty.

What is particularly interesting are the elements of fascination and mystery that continue to cloak this land of warring tribes, handsome sunburnt men in turbans and beautiful village belles in their amazing skirts and mantles in rainbow colours. It is as if the spirit colours the sands of the desert, bringing it alive for all time.

The western section consists mainly of the sandy wastes of the formidable Thar desert. The mud forts of hardy tribes speak of a valiant courage even as gaily bedecked women behind a sparse veil continue with the chores of housewives familiar to women all over the world. In the northern regions, the desert has been irrigated and reclaimed into fertile tracts. But it is the eastern desert section, dominated by the Aravalli range of mountains, that gives us a truly decorative and romantic people.

Princely rambles: History and pageantry crowd the capital city of Jaipur, the pink tinted, walled city built in 1727 by Maharaja Jai Singh. A great astronomer, the Maharaja also built the Jantar Mantar observatory for collecting scientific data. The Hawa Mahal Palace is an exotic extravaganza built in 1799, where scores of latticed windows overhang each other in a honeycomb of screens over five storeys high. In the city, scientifically planned and laid by the chief architect, Vidyadhar, according to the norms prescribed in the Hindu architectural treatise, *Shilpa-Shastra,* the City Palace is beautifully positioned in the centre of the capital, surrounded by gardens, and growing outwards in tiers into separate administrative and residential sections according to people's professions. Vidyadhar is believed to have cleared the drawings of all home - facades personally.

Exquisite palaces, forts, water tanks and pavilions are to be found in the wooded mountain site of 17th century Amber, the older capital which was replaced by Jaipur. Amber brings alive the beauty of traditional Rajput capitals, and it is said even Emperor Akbar coveted its beauty. Guarded on its higher reaches by Jaigarh and Nahargarh forts, Amber too is fortified, and an elephant ride up is a fascinating experience.

To one end of Jaipur lie Kota and Bundi, former princely settlements that have come to be known for the beautiful paintings that adorn the fort and palace walls. But a whole region that has become famous for its frescoes and wall paintings is Shekhawati. Visitors can begin their journey to Shekhawati in Samode, roughly an hour's drive from Jaipur, where the former palace with its rich array of paintings (the Durbar Hall is stunning) has become a hotel. From here, enroute to Delhi, they will drive through a region that was once home to merchants who built traditionally structured *havelis* and ordered them covered with frescoes that dealt with religious, social or secular themes. The adornments covered facades, draped pillars, decorated windows, pavilions, balconies and arches. It was a simple, unstructured school, and often the artists were led to paint objects and things they had only heard of, but never seen.

Also an extension from Jaipur is the wildlife park

of Ranthambhor, a sanctuary where the tiger is a familiar figure. One of the country's finest parks, it is known for its large population of deer.

Romance and chivalry: The lake-city of Udaipur is beautiful beyond description. The mountains nestle close to the blue waters of Pichola lake and provide a perfect setting for the stunning Jag Nivas Palace (now the Lake Palace hotel) in the centre of the lake and the exotic peacock mosaics of the Maharana's palace and the Jag Mandir Palace. Considered to be an oriental dream, Udaipur has ridden the crest of western imagination for long.

All around Udaipur, artificial lakes, water tanks, ornamental pools interspersed with white marble temples, shrines and palaces remain as relics of their antiquity — as much at home in their unchanged surroundings then as now.

North of Udaipur is the famous pilgrim site of Nathdwara where the 12th century temple of Lord Krishna defied attempts by Muslim invaders to carry away the sculptured images. The historic pass of Haldighati, 41 miles from Udaipur, is another relic of

bravery where Rajput soldiers died almost to a man while defending their land against the Mughal might of Akbar.

East of Udaipur is Chittaurgarh, an eighth century citadel built atop a 500 foot high hill. Tales of impossible courage are corroborated by historical facts. Commanding strategical superiority, it offered repeated resistance to furious onslaughts by the Mughal armies till it finally succumbed to their siege. Chittaur saw so much bloodshed in its defence, it has always remained a heroic symbol of Rajput valour.

Along with Meherangarh and Chittaurgarh, Kumbhalgarh is ranked as one of the three great hill-forts of Rajasthan. The Kumbhalgarh fort is perched high, a handsome edifice, well structured and built to provide protection. Its battlements pierce the sky from its hilltop ramble, and the few visitors to this great *garh* tell of the ignorance of one of Rajashthan's most historic sites.

West of Udaipur, 70 miles at most, is the plateau-hill resort of Mount Abu, famed for the 11th century Dilwara temples — a Jain religious stronghold. Pure white marble, richly decorated, reflects the genius in sculptured art.

Desert splendour: The town of Jodhpur on the edge of the Thar desert lies on a low ridge of sandstone hills. Its commanding position notwithstanding, the town of Jodhpur is encircled by a virtually impregnable stone wall built in 1458. A great fort on a high escarpment can be approached only through regal doorways. A magnificent panorama of miles of sandy desert is matched by the exquisite palaces in the citadel and the many temples around. More remarkable is the continuation of a centuries old life-style within these citadels – quiet, untouched by the march of modernisation in other parts of India. An ironic footnote here is a reference to the internationally accepted *Jodhpuris* (riding breeches) originating here which have left an indelible contribution in international equestrian dress codes.

Jaisalmer, in the heart of the Thar desert, is another ancient citadel atop a rocky hillrise, protected by a massive three-mile wall and enclosing elaborately decorated palaces, temples and fort embattlements. The striking part is the yellow stone used everywhere which blends with the sands of the desert and turns a magical silver hue on moonlit nights. An excellent library houses rare 12th century palm leaf manuscripts in wooden covers. Also of note are some remarkable Jain shrines. A sea of sand surrounds Jaisalmer and isolates it from civilization, yet this caravan trade-route town has seen the flowering of some of the strongest *haveli*-architecture in all Rajasthan. The sandstone *havelis* are exquisitely patterned with stone screen windows, pavilions and balconies.

Bikaner is yet another fiery medieval citadel with superb palaces, forts, temples and mosques. Red and yellow sandstone etch formidable edifices. The 16th century Jungarh Fort is lavishly decorative, some of the royal apartments within painted beautifully. The embellishments include glass mosaics, gilt reliefs, fine lattice work in stone, intricate mirrors and decorative arches. Red sandstone structures dot the countryside. Jain temples belonging to the 16th century are richly carved in and around Bikaner. Of more recent origin is the Lallgarh Palace, a western interpretation , in red sandstone, of a Rajput residence. Close to Bikaner is the former shooting retreat, Gajner, while on another flank of the city is Deshnoke with its marble temple dedicated to rats.

The other desert city of Ajmer holds a strategic importance because it commands the northern approach to the desert. This ancient city has shrines of great significance to Muslim and Hindu devotees.

Pages 74-75: A rider trots across the race course in the heart of Calcutta; to the background is the Victoria Memorial, a magnificent marble building raised to honour the Queen Empress of India and inaugurated in 1921 by the Prince of Wales. In teeming Calcutta, time has stood still at Victoria Memorial, and the Raj lurks in the shadows of its stately corridors.

Pages 76-77: Women from erstwhile royal homes swirl to the graceful beat of the 'ghummar' dance. On occasions such as weddings, the people of Rajasthan dress in their traditional clothes, and in a segregated enclave the women set durbar where song and dance is a distinctive feature.

Page 79: Jaisalmer's most lasting influence on the state has been its architecture. Here, the Patwon ki Haveli represents the mansions of the rich traders of centuries past who had their homes ordered to rival those of richer principalities within the state. Since Jaisalmer controlled the trade routes, it controlled money and could therefore, buy the finest available talent. The result is havelis with a wealth of details in the carvings and screens that front their facades, keep the homes in cool shadows and allow in breezes even at the hottest point of the day.

Opposite page: The Hawa Mahal in Jaipur is one of the city's most often photographed royal buildings. However, the Hawa Mahal is not truly a palace, its honeycomb structure cleverly designed to allow in cooling breezes and still afford privacy to women of the royal house when viewing state processions and street activities. It was built in the 19th century by the poet king Sawai Pratap Singh as a house of worship for Radha-Krishna.

It has been the seat of power for various Rajput and Mughal kings and overlords. Its colourful, though violent, history speaks of a series of wars. While the shrine of the Muslim saint Khwaja Muin-ud-Din Chisti, a delicate and beautiful structure, attracts thousands of believers, the holy waters of the Pushkar Lake make it a sacred pilgrim spot for Hindus and command a spectacular following. The Pushkar festival is now internationally famous and visitors are struck by the stark beauty and raw magnificence of this great land.

It is relatively recently that the smaller towns of Alwar – a Rajput fortification famous for its invaluable museum of fine Rajasthani miniature paintings, an illuminated copy of the Koran, and an armoury containing gold studded weapons of Mughal emperors – and Deeg, a sumptuous garden city dotted with ornamental pools and channels and romantic palaces inlaid with precious stone – have come to the attention of visitors.

The town of Bharatpur is famous for its fort laid by the successful Jat leader Suraj Mal. However, its claim to international recognition lies in the Keoladeo Ghana bird sanctuary, a superb natural reserve for migratory birds like the rare Siberian crane. The swampy area of the reserve, criss-crossed with dykes and water channels, is extremely rich in its natural bio-reserves and habitat for all kinds of water birds, and its unique eco-system has made it a naturalist's dream. The Sariska Game Sanctuary between Delhi and Jaipur is an excellent tiger reserve with thick jungle foliage rich in flora and fauna.

The story of a Rajasthan tour would not be complete without a keepsake to take back. Rajasthani handicrafts produce an amazing range of needlework, embroidery, mirror work, bead and glass and lac bangles and other ornamentation, fine leather and wood products and excellent inlay work in gold jewellery, wood and brass.

Opposite page: *Rajasthanis conduct themselves with a bearing and grace that is the result of centuries of living in the desert with a fiercely independent spirit. Their turbans ignite the desert with colour and provide them with a protective shield against the sun.*

Above: *Women wear long skirts, blouses and a mantle in a hue of colours, in turn sequinned, embroidered and appliqued so their dress is dazzling; their accoutrements too are splendid – bangles on the hands, the glint of silver and gold at ankle, elbow and throat – even if it is for a session of gossip.*

Preceding pages: *Despite the aridity of the desert, there are still pools of water available close to community settlements. Deep water wells provide drinking water which often has to be carried over long distances to meet the needs of homesteads. Here, a woman washes her clothes in the shadow of the Ghagron fortress in Jhalawar.*

Above: *Festive occasions are colourful affairs, especially so if they are connected with royalty. Here, the head of the former house of Jaipur holds court in formal attire on a special occasion when even the elephant is caparisoned to suit the mood of the occasion.*

*Dancers of the 'sapera' community have an
exceptional talent for music and dance. This woman
performs at the Samode Palace near Jaipur in a swirl of skirts,
attended by rhythmic beat.*

Preceding pages: *Sonar Qila or the 'golden fort' in Jaisalmer rises like a mirage from the desert sands, its ramparts blending with the undulating sand dunes. Jaisalmer is the 12th century capital of the Bhatti Rajputs who shifted here from Lodurva and built themselves fortifications to ensure their hegemony in the region.*

Above: *Meherangarh fort crowns a sheer base, making its five hundred year old ramparts impregnable. A Rathore stronghold, Rao Jodha shifted his capital from nearby Mandore when seeking additional defence installations for his principality.*

*The formidable ramparts of Meherangarh evoke the feudal
cry of the 'Ran Banka Rathores' but within, the palaces are
delicately detailed with screens, arches, pavilions and stained
glass windows, for essentially the Rajput warrior and
chieftain is a romantic at heart, and an aesthete.*

Preceding pages: *In a land known for its chivalry, the ruins of the fortress of Chittaurgarh tell tales of unparalleled courage and an indomitable spirit of feudal independence. The fort fell to seiges in the 14th and the 16th centuries, the former because the Muslim sultan of Delhi wished to make the Chittaur princess his own, the latter resulting in a jauhar (mass suicide) that consigned 13,000 Rajput women to the flames.*

Above: *The annual Pushkar Mela close to Ajmer is a major trading, religious and social occasion in an event that is timeless and has been known to occur for centuries. Camel and livestock are traded, alliances fixed, gossip exchanged, homage paid at a Brahma temple and a dip taken in the holy waters of the Pushkar pond.*

Opposite page: *Jag Niwas appears to float on the blue waters of Lake Pichola in Udaipur. Built in 1746 as the summer residence of the rulers of Mewar, and now more famous as the internationally celebrated Lake Palace, this is but one of several other such royal retreats in the lake's waters.*

Follow the Coast

One of the most exotic ways of exploring India is to travel along her vast and varied coastline that stretches an amazing 3,000 km along the ocean front. In most parts, a parallel and picturesque road skirts the coastline, and while this may often not be the best in terms of maintenance, it offers the finest combination of a motor holiday along some of the best beaches and sea fronts anywhere in the world.

India's entire southern peninsula juts out into the sea and is skirted by a remarkable palm fringed coastline that runs all the way from the 'good country' of Saurashtra and Maharashtra in western India to the southern tip more than 1,200 km away to the tropical paradise of Kerala, around the tip at Kanyakumari commonly known as 'Land's End' and back up along the magic of the eastern coast to the historic port of Madras, French-Pondicherry and the Orissa sea front.

Of striking note is the fact that the lush coastline is not only dotted with ancient and defunct ports, modern harbours and ship building yards, but also temple towns with all the makings of great seaside cities of the past, modern beach resort complexes and metropolitan cities. As intriguing are the varied lifestyles reflected in different belts of the coastal region. Each area is intrinsically fused with the local customs, art and craft, and offers cultural forays into traditional strongholds.

In Gujarat: The journey along India's coastline begins, quixotically enough, at the Rann of Kutch – an extension of the Thar Desert. This salt encrusted wilderness is known for its astonishing variety of birdlife, in particular flamingos and pelicans; the wild ass that wanders in herds over this barren landscape is to be found only here in India.

As we go south across the Gulf of Kutch we come to Dwarka, celebrated by Hindus as the capital of Lord Krishna's empire. It is believed that the ancient city mentioned in Hindu texts actually lies beneath the sea, and some portions have been excavated and identified. The temple of Dwarkanath at this site is a big pilgrim draw. Sixty miles south along the coast is Porbandar, birthplace of Mahatma Gandhi and a popular resort.

Further down the coast one stops at a revered shrine that seems to step out of the sea. This is the legendary Somnath temple which was so richly and lavishly decorated that it was plundered and destroyed on three separate occasions by the marauding armies of different invaders.

A large number of intriguing port relics and temple towns dot this coastal road. East of Somnath is the magnificent Gir forest and sanctuary, home of the last of the magnificent Asian lions. Jungle trees stretch out towards the sea and make for a short but dramatic coastal strip. Besides its lions, the Gir is famous for its blue bulls, spotted deer, antelope and gazelles. Stepping inwards to the Gulf of Cambay is the once-famous port of Surat, a strategic trading port for the French, English and Dutch in the 17th century and now a smaller port of less importance, but with a number of good beaches around it. Smaller interior towns which are well worth a visit are Palitana, known for its excellent Jain architecture, and the sun-temple town of Modhera. A large number of beach resorts have been developed along the coast and these make for excellent overnight stops along the motorway.

The city of Ahmedabad with Cambay, its old seaport, is now the commercial centre of India's cotton industry. It was one of the more sophisticated

Pages 96-97: *Goa is known for its very fine beaches by the Arabian Sea, and for its Indo-Portuguese temperament. Calangute beach is one of the most popular, and was the first to be discovered by the 'flower children' of the '70s.*

Preceding page: *An image of Shiva sculpted into the rock cut caves of Ellora some ten centuries ago. Thirty four rock cut caves were carved out of the hillside and sculpted with Buddhist, Jain and Hindu images in a marvellous feat to create one of the historically most enduring Indian monuments.*

Above: *Just as Ellora is celebrated for its sculptures, Ajanta is known for the high quality of it tempera paintings in thirty Buddhist caves that recount the tales of Buddhist legends, and of the Buddha. Ajanta and Ellora are a cathedral of high art of the medieval ages.*

Opposite page: *The Gateway of India on Bombay's waterfront was built as a triumphal arch commemorating the 1911 visit of King George V for the famous Delhi Durbar. Made of basalt rock, the Gateway welcomed and saw off senior British officials who came by sea, and is today the site from where motor-launches ferry passengers on an hour long ride to Elephanta island with its grand rock cut cave sculptures.*

cities of the 15th and 17th centuries and has a number of spendid Indo-Saracenic buildings and Muslim monuments. But not all Ahmedabad's highlights are of the distant past. It was here, by the banks of the Sabarmati, that Gandhi established his ashram. In more recent times, the city has become celebrated for its offbeat museums, such as those devoted exclusively to calico textiles, kites or the folk arts. A wealthy city, Ahmedabad also has a skyline marked by the works of some major architects such as Le Corbusier or Louis Kahn.

The town of Baroda, now called Vadodara, green and lush in the heart of banyan plantations, is a well planned, spacious city, famous as a centre for arts, crafts, and the study of various subjects. It is also known for its museums and the Oriental Institute of Research.

Bombay and Around: A great Indian city on the west coast is metropolitan Bombay – India's commercial nerve centre. It is not only India's most affluent city, it is also the busiest international arrival and departure point, both by air and sea. Its port handles half of the country's total sea trade. Its seven

mile wide natural harbour makes it one of the best ports of the world.

Bombay has a romantic past. It was spread originally over seven islands and in 1534 was ceded to the Portuguese by the Shah of Gujarat. It changed hands when it was given as part of Catherine of Braganza's dowry to Charles II of England in 1662. He, in turn, leased it to the East India Company for the kingly sum of £ 10 annually.

Bombay's seven islands are no longer distinguishable. It has grown into a sprawling commercial city which not only supports a thriving sea industry but reflects the economic pace of progress in the country. The Prince of Wales Museum near the docks has a superb collection of Oriental fine arts, particularly jade, textiles and European and Indian paintings. Down picturesque Marine Drive, a delightful seaside promenade; the Chowpatty and Juhu beaches, known for their evening strollers and the *bhelpuri* snack – a light, tasty meal, flavoured by the moist sea air of Bombay; and the suburbs of Bandra, and the city's sea-front is complete.

The Hanging Gardens and Victoria Gardens are picturesque botanical forays with a zoo and museum to boot. These are among the few escapes from the crush of the city into the limited isles of tranquillity they offer.

From the yellow-basalt landmark of Bombay, the Gateway of India, which commands the harbour, there is a boat trip 10 km out into the sea to the Elephanta Islands, famous for their eighth century temples and rock-cut statues in huge stone caves carved from the mountainside. But on mainland Bombay, travellers will have to fit in to what best fits their mould. For Bombay is a lively city. One day it might be exhibiting contemporary artists at its Victoria Terminus railway station; another day celebrating the anniversary of a superstar's films; yet another, engrossed in celebrating its mega-festival, Ganesh Chaturthi. Round the clock, the city hums, pulses, alive, a sea of creativity and an ode to metro survival.

Bombay, traditionally known as India's city of streets paved with gold – not to mention dreams – is home also to India's enormous film industry. Its studios, film-star glamour and extravagant life styles are reminiscent of Hollywood in the west, adding to its attraction as a city that sells fantasies, and earning it the nickname 'Bollywood' from the irreverent scribes who chart the rise and fall of Indian film stars with unvarying zeal.

Above: *Goa in the 16th century came under Portuguese dominion and its Iberian influence suited the people and the countryside. The churches that came up revealed Gothic and Renaissance baroque schools of architecture. The Cathedral of Bom Jesus with its laterite exterior and gilded interiors, enshrines the remains of St Francis Xavier, and is today a National Heritage site.*

A visit to Bombay is incomplete without an excursion inland to the Ajanta and Ellora caves which are renowned for a collection of thirty-four Hindu and Jain cave temples at Ellora, and thirty Buddhist monasteries at Ajanta which date as far back as the second century. This display of art and human spirit takes on a magnificent form in the rock-cut caves which have been carved into the stone face of boulder-mountains. Mere genius is an insufficient description of the craftsmen of this era; how they achieved the gargantuan task of cutting away some three million cubic feet of rock to produce the superb Kailasa temple at Ellora is impossible to visualise. This vast sculpted temple, in fact, contains a gateway, a pavilion, assembly hall, inner sanctum and even a tower — all of it hewn out of stone, in beautiful designs of remarkable delicacy.

Ajanta's is a more picturesque location, since the stone hill out of which the thirty Buddhist monasteries are cut overlooks a gorge, at the bottom of which flows a rivulet. Each temple cave is distinct in its artist's rendering of sculpted forms and delicate tracery. These caves are renowned the world over for their tempera paintings, often wrongly described as frescoes, many of which retain still the luminosity of their original colours. The paintings are rich, well tempered and show an advanced understanding of every aspect of art, be it proportion, balance or colour.

Excursion trips from Bombay can be planned to Aurangabad, two hundred miles northeast, which once flourished, in the 17th century, as capital of the Deccan kingdoms of Emperor Aurangzeb's Mughal empire, and is known for a beautiful marble mausoleum, Bibi-Ka-Maqbara. As a matter of fact, Ellora is a mere eighteen miles northwest of Aurangabad, and Ajanta sixty-seven miles north of the city. Aurangabad-Ellora-Ajanta can be put together as a mini-circuit in addition to a planned itinerary of a visit to Bombay.

Also in the vicinity of Bombay is the popular hill resort of Mahabaleshwar, once the summer capital of the government of Bombay. Beautiful woods, valleys and mountain streams at 4,000 ft above sea level make for a charming holiday.

A quiet, tranquil city further to the interior is Poona — now called Pune — which enjoys fine weather all year round, and is the home of the prestigious National Defence Academy; in addition, it has the distinction of being the Indian headquarters of the world-famous religious movement of the Rajneesh Ashram. The Raja Kelkar Museum houses some delightful exhibits, such as musical instruments, oil lamps, strange locks and betel-nut cutters, in an

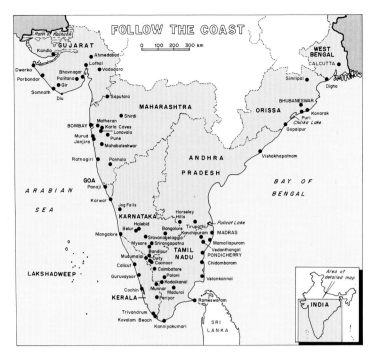

exhibition put together by a single individual.

The Karla and Bhaja caves provide another interesting detour, 126 km south-east of Bombay. A beautiful cave temple at Karla, more than 2,000 years old, is an instance of astonishing purity of design. A 'sun window' filters light into the interior of the cave onto sculpted figures of women, elephant heads and back-to-back lions; of the Bhaja caves on a lush hill, an attractive *chaitya,* or temple cave, dating back to 200 B.C., is the most significant.

Beach country: Moving along the coast, 250 miles south of Bombay is the beach paradise of Goa which stretches 35 miles east to west and 60 miles north to south. This beautiful coastal enclave divides Maharashtra state in the north from Karnataka in the south. From this tiny state, one sees the gentle rise of land into the strong, bold hills, known as the Western Ghats, that stand sentinel on the shores of the Arabian Sea all along its coastline to the south.

The ancient port of Old Goa was an important trading post for Arab merchants in the 15th century. It changed hands and came under Portuguese rule in 1510, after which it developed into a great port for trade between Europe and the Far East. In time, Goa became the capital of the Portuguese eastern colonies, and absorbed the architecture, religion and lifestyle of Portugal.

Reverting to India as late as 1961, Goa retains a delightful flavour of Portuguese culture which gives it a unique charm. The main features of Goa are the natural exuberance of its local people, their passion for song and dance, their local drink, *feni*, which is distilled from its cash crops — coconut and cashew —

and a mouth-watering choice in the selection and preparation of gourmet seafood; and, of course, the sea. Miles upon miles of golden, virgin sand, fringed by coconut or cashew palm trees, blue waters that are ideal for swimming and water sports, sunny, clear skies and gentle weather conditions combine to create the perfect holiday destination.

Also on offer is a plethora of sightseeing, and even the shortest itinerary must include visits to the Basilica of Bom Jesus, which houses the mortal remains of St. Francis Xavier; the magnificent Church of the Immaculate Conception in the heart of Panjim, Goa's capital city; Mangueshi temple in the north; Pilar Seminary; and the colourful bustle of Friday market at Mapusa. Once known as the 'Pearl of the Orient', Goa continues to be celebrated for its traditional homes, its laid-back lifestyle (which includes an afternoon siesta) and its annual carnival, three days of fun and frolic, during which the *feni* flows even more abundantly than usual, and the streets resound with costumed revellers' shouts of 'Viva Carnaval!'.

Dedicated sun-worshippers will discover two of Goa's best beaches – Baga and Calangute – to its north, and the fine resorts of Dona Paula and Colva to the south. A large number of imaginatively styled chalets, hotels and five star resorts dot the entire state, catering to every type of holiday-maker in the inimitable tradition of Goan hospitality.

Down the coast are a number of good beaches and small ports from Goa to the next big stop at Mangalore. Karwar has several excellent beaches – all of them secluded and quiet – and is only a short distance from Goa. Ankola is the next beach village, with some attractive 15th century historic ruins near the main highway. Harvanthe, Malpe, has some good fishing, and 5 km down the coast is Udipi, with its apron-sized beach and the beautiful 13th century Shri Krishna temple. Ullal beach is clean, has safe, warm waters, and is close to the port town of Mangalore.

The scenic mountainous coastal area of Coorg lies south-west of Karnataka and borders the state of Kerala. It is a bountiful, lush territory, known as a coffee growing base. The capital of Coorg is the sleepy hill town of Mercara, 124 km west of Mysore. Close by is the Nagarhole wildlife sanctuary, known for its rich wildlife and thick jungles.

Our next stop along the coast is the once great seaport of Mangalore which was a strategic axis to erstwhile empires in this region. It was a major sea outlet for trade in coffee and cashewnut with foreign sea merchants. Today it is a centre for trade in coffee and cashewnut, though its importance as a port has diminished. Mangalore is also an important rail and road junction for travel to Goa, Bangalore, Trivandrum and even far-off Delhi.

An attractive picnic spot is Jog Falls close to the coast – the most dramatic and possibly the highest falls in the country – a 253 metres drop in four separate falls.

Along the Malabar Coast and into the backwaters: From Mangalore the coastal belt begins to take on a fresh, green, tangy colour as the vegetation gets thicker, and lusher. Soon enough you are in the 'magic-green' state of Kerala, a tropical paradise of backwater lagoons and a network of canals, tea, rubber and coconut plantations and endless fields of sap-green rice seedlings. The blue seas of Kerala are legendary for they appear bluer than elsewhere, its sandy beaches whiter because of the deep green swaying palms that form a thick belt along the coast, and its history – quite without exception – surprising.

Facing the Arabian Sea is a short strip of coast, known in the past as the great Malabar coast, dominated by 5,000 feet high mountains that are rich in forest, timber, cardamom, pepper, coffee, ginger, turmeric and a host of other crops and spices that have earned it the sobriquet of the 'spice kingdom'.

The Malabar coast was a byword in ancient times for exotic trade of a cosmopolitan nature. King Solomon's ships are said to have paid a visit here in 1,000 BC, not to mention Greek and Roman galleys, Chinese junks and Arabian dhows. Christian sects, the Portuguese, Syrians and even an entire Jewish settlement exist to this day in Kerala. To this melting-pot one can add the martial race of the Nayars, and the great classical dance form – Kathakali – which has its origin here.

Trivandrum, which appears almost at the end of India's southern tip, is the capital of Kerala. Built on seven hills, Trivandrum is a dignified city, characterised by a beautiful, low skyline, red tiled roofs and small winding lanes lined with coconut and palm trees. The Shri Padmanabhaswamy Temple and the Napier Museum are well worth a visit. Dominating Trivandrum, though at some distance from the city, is the beautiful Kovalam beach, now on the international itinerary of beach watchers. Kovalam was once the summer resort of the Maharaja of Travancore whose palace atop a hill overlooks the ocean waters: today, a five star beach complex provides a pleasant retreat. The distinct character of the Kerala countryside lends Kovalam

and other tropical beaches in this area an
unparalleled charm; their natural setting is exotic
and quite unspoilt.

Between Trivandrum and Mangalore, along the
Malabar Coast, is the port town of Calicut where
Vasco da Gama first landed in 1498 and which
subsequently became an area of turmoil as warring
colonial rulers – such as the British and the Dutch –
vied for supremacy. It was a centre for cotton
production in its heyday, hence the English 'calico'.
Today it is a sleepy port with rich plantations of
pepper, sandalwood and coconut.

Cochin is built along a narrow peninsula and a
group of islands. Its antiquity is reflected in streets
which offer a view of Portuguese houses built almost
five hundred years ago, Chinese fishing nets against
the ocean front, brought in originally from the
courts of Kublai Khan, a Jewish community around a
16th century synagogue, and the beautiful
Mattancherry Palace built for the Raja of Cochin. The
city remains a major naval base, a great sea port and
a modern ship building yard. It has a pleasant old
world charm, and its homes, lifestyle and traditional

Preceding pages: *The Jewish synagogue in Cochin is one of
the oldest in the country, and its interior can best be described
as lavish. Cantonese tiles embellish it, representative of the
Chinese influence on Kerala. It also enjoyed the support of the
Travancore royals. India today has only a very small
population of Jews left.*

Above: *Performances of Kathakali are commonplace in
Kerala, where this illustrative dance with its elaborate face
make-up masks often takes a few hours to put on. Other than
Kathakali, the coastal state with its high literacy rate has
given rise to the Mohiniattam dance and the Kalaripayattu
martial arts tradition.*

settlements belong to a leisurely past.

The area around Cochin is interesting and remarkably attractive. Alleppey, Kottayam and Quilon are exotic names in an equally exotic background. The backwaters of Kerala are the highlight of a visit to this state. Quilon to Alleppey is connected by an unforgettable waterway which offers an unusual holiday. It takes you in straw-roofed country boats along palm fringed lagoons, canals, lakes and waterways which put on view a slice of life that is quite unknown to most travellers. From among coconut and palm fronds, red tiled homes peep out, Chinese fishing nets dry along sparkling blue lakes, and dugouts carrying coir, cashewnut and other goods ply narrow, overhanging shady canals. Along the wider open stretches of water, the more dramatic boats with enormous sails and dragon-shaped prows seem to step out of a different century and lend a feeling of strangeness as though transposed in time. Altogether, the backwaters of Kerala offer a fascinating, interesting cruise.

Quilon, one must remember, has been a port since Phoenician times, 3,000 years ago. Alleppey is the home of the world famous snake boat races — a dramatic sight, not to be missed — held every August, when a large number of low slung dugouts with decorated sterns and as many as a hundred rowers in each boat, compete in the races. It is a great event in Kerala, and one of the most exciting sights in all the world.

A visit to the Periyar Game Sanctuary, from Trivandrum or Quilon, or wherever else you might be in Kerala, is a must. The 300 sq mile sanctuary is extensive and located in the higher reaches of a hilly tract. An enormous lake studded with dried wood stumps of trees on which a rich array of birdlife suns, and thick jungles all around, where wild elephants, big game, deer, and a cross section of wildlife can be viewed, make for a great outing. Of interest is the fact that game viewing is done by motor launch alone. Mention must be made of Varkala, 32 miles north of Trivandrum, a great pilgrim spot for Hindus on account of the Janardhan temple. Varkala has a picturesque beach backed by red cliffs and mineral water streams running down the cliff sides.

Land's End and coastal temples: Kanyakumari, or Cape Comorin, is literally Land's End of the Indian subcontinent and forms the cup of the southernmost tip of the mainland. In this pleasant spot a rocky beach is pounded by high waters and a promenade runs along the coast in the city limits. Here the Bay of Bengal meets the waters of the Indian Ocean, and on a full moon night one can see the sun set and the moon rise simultaneously on the majestic waters of the ocean front. The temple of Kanyakumari is a favourite pilgrim spot; so also the Vivekananda Memorial, built on two rocky islands about 200 metres from the shore in honour of the great Indian philosopher-saint. Between Trivandrum and Kanyakumari is the charming Kolachal beach.

Taking the curve up on the eastern coast, one arrives at the pilgrimage centre of Rameswaram. On an island in the Gulf of Mannar is this small town, famous for its 12th century Ramanathaswamy temple with its elaborate carvings and magnificent corridors, one of which is said to measure 4,000 feet or 1,220 metres in length. Coral reefs and small palm fringed beaches round off the island and add to its attraction.

Pondicherry, further up the eastern coast, is a former 18th century French settlement which the French voluntarily gave up in the 1950s. This quiet seaside city has absorbed far less French culture than Goa has its Portuguese origins. What sets Pondicherry apart is the Sri Aurobindo Ashram and the township of Auroville — an experiment in international living — and the lovely natural beaches, seaside breezes and soothing climate of a well-located settlement.

Continuing up the coast about 40 miles is the astonishing Nataraja temple, built in the ninth century at Chidambaram. Dedicated to Shiva, the cosmic dancer, the temple bears 108 different postures of classical Indian dance. Of particular beauty is a large court 340 feet in length and 190 feet in width, punctuated with a thousand pillars.

Close to Chidambaram is the old Danish port of Tranquebar which, from 1620 to 1840, was a stronghold of Denmark. The settlement has a well preserved castle, not to mention a fort, churches and old colonial houses.

Opposite page, top: Chinese fishing nets frame the skyline and the sea in Cochin. Kerala is a major spice growing state, and its prized plantations were the reason for its sea-trade with all important nations who valued its exotic spices. The result was major international influences that have given this coastal state much of its unique character.

Opposite page, bottom: The Bay of Bengal washes ashore at Palam, an old harbour enroute to the holy town of Rameswaram.

Further up the coast is the once great harbour and naval centre of the Pallava empire which ruled 1,200 years ago – Mahabalipuram or Mammallapuram. Today this town is better known for its breathtaking sculptured works, the surviving Shore Temple, built in the seventh century and dedicated to Lord Vishnu, and as a remarkably fine beach resort – one of the best along the entire eastern coast.

Mahabalipuram is also known as the 'city of the seven pagodas or *rathas'*. Superb sculptures adorn entire walls of the *rathas* – bas reliefs, pastoral scenes, panel upon panel of the epic fight between Durga and the demon, Mahishasura, and a series of stone frescoes that seem to spring free of their stone bearings. Arjuna's penance is the most impressive and possibly the world's largest bas-relief – 80 feet in length and 20 feet in height.

Mahabalipuram's piece de resistance is its superb and unbroken beach that extends from the dark stone Shore Temple, rising in a wreath of breaking waves all the way along the coast, 45 km to Madras. Dotted along the beach are a series of comfortable resorts at some distance from each other which

gives the beach a fine sense of privacy.

Southern capital and gateway: Madras, India's fourth largest city, is the cradle of India's civilization, and the feeling of grace and dignity in the city and its environs cannot be ignored. Madras is one of the few cities which has a beach – the setting is in the heart of the city – and extends as one of the longest beaches in the world for more than eight miles from Adyar in the south to Madras harbour in the north – the famed Marina beach.

Five hundred years ago the Portuguese came to Madras and formed the first European settlement. It is believed that Thomas the Apostle was the first missionary to land in AD 78. Fort St. George stands testimony to the colonial struggle for India between the British and the French in the 18th century. Modern Madras has sprung up around the Fort which also houses an Anglican church that dates back to 1680. A series of historic relics dot the city – the houses of Clive, the Duke of Wellington, and Elihu Yale. Interspersed are such paradoxes as the Snake Park and the Crocodile Conservation Centre. Not content, the city boasts two superb Hindu

Opposite page: *In the Arabian Sea, motor launches cross the river Mandovi close to the capital, Panaji, while a Goan church peeps out of the lush coastal treeline.*

Above: *Carrot and radish transporters wash their produce before loading it into trucks in the southern hill resort, Ooty. Established by the British, the resort is often referred to as 'Snooty Ooty' and has rambling colonial bungalows, hotels and mansions.*

temples, Kapaleeswarar and Parthasarathy, dating back to the eighth century.

Madras has won acclaim as the home of vegetarian cuisine and its food style is distinct and succulent. It is also deservedly famous for its superb silks and handicrafts. But more than anything else, the city is known to art lovers the nation over for its music and dance *sabhas*. Traditions here are cherished, and Kalakshetra is one of the best of the schools where the Bharatnatyam dance form is imparted to an eager body of students. An excursion to Kanchipuram, the golden city, is not to be missed. There are as many as 124 shrines, some of the older ones dating back 1,200 years. These have painted murals on entire walls, and sculptures and bas reliefs decorating pillars and roofs. Kanchipuram is also known for its master craftsmen who weave a particularly famous design in silk, aptly known as Kanjeevaram.

En route to Kanchipuram is a hill some 500 feet high atop which is a modest temple dedicated to Lord Shiva. Here, two white kites come in regularly to be fed by the head priest and are believed to be the spirit of two saints. This phenomenon has been known to occur for several generations, and is recorded in early histories. The place is called Thirukalikuram.

The Andhra coast: From Madras up north into the Andhra Pradesh coastline which stretches all of 600 miles along the Bay of Bengal. Much of the coast is dotted with rocky wastes, sandy swamps and intensely cultivated hinterlands. The first major stop along this coast is the resort town of Waltair which has a fine climate and an equally fine beach, several kilometres of fine sandy beach and some picturesque rocks and sparkling blue pools. On account of its relative inaccessibility, Waltair remains a seaside resort of immense beauty that is not yet exploited.

Adjoining Waltair to the south is the commercial and industrial hub of the entire region, Vishakhapatnam. This is presently India's premier ship building centre and, after Madras, the most important port of the south. The beach at Vishakhapatnam is excellent, and a number of good resorts have come up on the shoreline as a result.

Crossing over into the state of Orissa which lies

Opposite page: *The piece de resistance of Mahabalipuram, the 7th century port city of the Pallavas, are rock cut monoliths, the best known of which, on account of the fine sculpturing that follows the contours of the rocks and includes a fissure into its grand plan, is Arjuna's Penance, alternatively known as the Descent of Ganga.*

Above: *The seaside Sun Temple of Konark in Orissa is a marvellous feat of architectural skill and was often referred to as the Black Pagoda by ancient mariners. Built in the 13th century with 1,200 artisans toiling for 16 years to execute its fine details, the monument is represented as the chariot of the sun god drawn by seven horses and with twelve exquisitely sculpted wheels. The Sun Temple is one of the masterpieces of Indian art.*

along the eastern seaboard of India, one comes across a fertile country and exotic tribals who have managed to retain most of their ancient rites and rituals.

The first step as we climb north from Vishakhapatnam along the coast is likely to be the charmingly named, quiet seaside resort of Gopalpur-on-Sea. Nestled at the foot of a picturesque range of cliffs, Gopalpur offers a fine beach, the sight of charming village belles and men of the fishing community and, most surprising of all, a western deluxe hotel.

Orissa's beachside temples: Close by, and a big draw, is the attractive Chilka Lake, an estuary of the Bay of Bengal and an excellent bird sanctuary for migratory birds. The setting itself is memorable. Thickly wooded hills of the Eastern Ghats dip into the enormous lake which is 45 miles (70 km) long, 10 miles (15 km) wide and is dotted with small islands. Quite naturally, water-sports, bird watching, fishing and hunting are activities that thrive in this land of abundance.

From these peaceful, sleepy coastal villages one reaches Puri on the coast. One of India's four holy cities, Puri celebrates the cult of Lord Vishnu and is venerated by Hindus. The temple of the Lord of the Universe — Jagannath — belongs to the 12th century and is an example of superb sculptures and paintings in the traditional style. What brings the world's focus on this small coastal town is the annual Rath Yatra or Car Festival when a million pilgrims converge on the town to watch the spectacle of devotees pulling the 16-foot high giant chariot which carries the images of Vishnu through the main streets of Puri to Gaundicha Mandir or Garden House. For the visitor in search of lazier pursuits, a beach holiday on Puri's seashore is on the cards. The sea waters are safe for bathing, though the waters can be rough. White sandy beaches fringed by dark woods at one end and glistening blue waters at the other are a big attraction.

Thirty km further east along the coast is Konark, where the magnificent ruins of the Sun Temple stand astride silver sand dunes. Conceived as a chariot for the Sun God, this remarkable 13th century temple has 24 gigantic stone wheels laboriously and delicately carved.

Of the temple sculptures that still remain, the figures of men and women in erotic poses — blissfully unaware of everything except their own exuberance — and dancers and musicians, seem almost to move, so striking is the artist's mastery over his medium.

There is a remote but excellent beach at Konark and together with the effect of the sun setting on the blackened Sun Temple, often referred to as the 'Black Pagoda' — a lonesome temple in the sand dunes which 1,200 sculptors are said to have worked upon for twelve years — a beach holiday takes on a different meaning.

From Puri inland to the capital of Orissa — Bhubaneswar — one begins a journey into the 'cathedral city' of India where more than a hundred exquisitely carved temples put on display the best of Indian art. The sculptures, reliefs and detailed and intricate stone carving are awe-inspiring. Of special note is the Lingaraja temple dominating a complex of temples that are beautifully decorated with figures in various explicit and erotic designs. The 12th century Rajrani temple is built on a grand scale and its proportions are said to be so perfect and so well-balanced that it is an instance of the greatest outpouring of sacred architecture anywhere in the world. The Ocean Drop or Bindusagar tank, the eighth century Parasurameswara and Mukteswara temples are other instances of excellent sculpted forms and purity of design.

At every instance, Bhubaneswar has an ancient ruin, a relic, a leftover temple site — so extravagant were its builders. Although the numbers today don't compare with the original 7,000 temples built here, they are in sufficient numbers to inspire the visitor. Bhubaneswar is also associated with the Buddhist sites of Dhauli, of a lion safari park at Simlipal, and with the development of a new city. A new capital (the earlier capital was Cuttack), it is still abuilding along a masterplan that will make it one of the most elegant among provincial capitals in the country.

In the Heartlands

There is an interesting circuit north of Delhi that gives the visitor a chance to partake of an essentially 'north-Indian' lifestyle — noisy, robust and rooted in the present. The 260 km route along the Grand Trunk Road from Delhi to Chandigarh typifies the circuit — it is one of the busiest highways in the country and the sheer volume and variety of commuting traffic is mind-boggling: trucks, buses, cars, motorcycles, scooters, jeeps, bullock-carts, cycle-rickshaws, cycles — anything on wheels qualifies for the ride.

Punjab: 92 km north is Panipat — the site of three great battles, each one of which changed the history of the country. Today there is little to remember the past by; instead, Panipat is a great centre for textile and cotton weaving.

Nestled among the foothills of the Sivalik range, Chandigarh, a post-Independence city, seems at odds with its typically Indian surroundings. Designed by Le Corbusier, with wide avenues, red brick houses and open spaces, it is pretty as a picture, and as unreal. The same careful planning is reflected in the attactive Pinjore gardens near Chandigarh. Designed by Fidai Khan, Emperor Aurangzeb's foster brother, the gardens centre around the Indo-Muslim architecture of the Shish Mahal Palace in marble and glass.

From here the next step is inevitably to Amritsar, the 'city which is a pool of nectar', where one finds the temple sacred to the Sikhs — the Golden Temple. Roofed over with gilded copper in 1802 by the Sikh Maharaja, Ranjit Singh, this astonishingly beautiful marble temple, built next to an enclosed pool which is considered sacred, is a holy site venerated by Hindus and Sikhs alike. Amritsar is today a bustling commercial centre for the state of Punjab and reflects the vibrant nature of its citizens, their distinct lifestyle and hospitality.

Nawabi elegance: South of Delhi one moves into the Indian heartlands. The capital of the state of Uttar Pradesh, Lucknow, a garden city, remains true to the spirit of its ancestors — it is a genteel, olde worlde city where breeding and refinement have been so deeply imbibed by its citizens that courtesy is their second nature and hospitality trimphs above all else. The 18th century capital of the Nawab-Wazirs and the stately Nawabs of Oudh, Lucknow was renowned as a gay, decadent and romantic city where Urdu poetry and an ornamental and lavish court held sway. Today it is easy to recapture this charm in the many musical and artistic shows that occur so often in the cultural belt of the city.

Lucknow boasts some buildings worth discovering. The Great Imambara, said to be the largest vaulted apartment in the world, is about 50 ft in height, and has no supporting columns. Ornamental gateways, corridors and galleries are highlights of this 18th century structure. As expected, the Muslims later built a small Imambara — a beautiful mausoleum with an ornate hall decorated with colourful stucco and gilt mirrors. Lofty minarets and huge domes of the royal mosque still call the faithful to prayer.

Beautiful 19th century tombs etch the Lucknow skyline. The main shopping area of the city is leisurely Hazrat Ganj where the famous Lucknow handicrafts — pure cotton weaves and handwoven thread embroidery called *chikan* and the fragrant Indian perfume *attar* — can be hand-picked.

Majesty and erotica: To the east, on one side of the Delhi-Lucknow circuit, and quie magnificent in their historic settings, Gwalior, Mandu and Khajuraho are attractions which, correctly speaking,

are in the middle of nowhere, but which can be visited while travelling between Agra and Lucknow. Yet, they form an invaluable link on India's most widely travelled circuit that begins at Delhi and includes Varanasi as its last link.

From Agra, head south to the thousand year old city of Gwalior with its legendary fort that rises 100 metres and dominates the city. The great fort reflects the drama of struggles between warring kingdoms to control it. It had continually changed hands from 1398 till 1858 – six centuries of power clashes beginning with the Tomar dynasty and ending with the British takeover.

The fort's walls are ten metres high and remain remarkably solid. A large number of imposing gates which served as strategic entrances, delightful palaces, temples and halls, take up the better part of a visit to Gwalior. The blue, green and gold palace of Man Singh, in particular, is a dainty four storeyed structure that seems to tilt its airy noise at the gaunt forbidding walls of the fort. The story of the brave Rani of Jhansi who was killed in a final assault by the British on this fort is remembered as a courageous

attempt to defend it, and wandering minstrels and bards sing songs that echo this story in the fort's cavernous halls. Shivpuri National Park, 72 miles away, is a wildlife haven where tiger and leopard can be spotted, though it is more usual to see deer species in the wilderness.

From Gwalior, it is a short journey to Khajuraho – the temple kingdom known for its creative genius from 950 AD. These superb temples built a thousand years ago by the Chandela kings are exceptionally well executed. A large number of temples and shrines dedicated to Vishnu, Parvati and Kali and Shiva mingle with the classic beauty of Jain temples, their spires rising into a blue sky. Among the finest examples of sculptures and wall carvings in India, the 22 temples display an amazing assortment of stone erotica. Nymphs, maidens, buxom women and athletic men engage in explicit sexual activities. The delicacy and finesse with which these sculptures have been executed have put them on par with the best art the world has to offer. Various interpretations have been offered on why these erotic carvings were sculpted in such fine detail, but none satisfactorily explains this Kamasutra in stone

Page 115: *The Shore Temple of Mahabalipuram, or Mamallapuram, a twin structure, considered one of the liveliest and most important monuments of the 7th century, is known for its structural strength despite the toll that saline erosion has taken on its basalt rock surface.*

Pages 116-117: *The Nihangs are martial Sikhs, and their celebrations at Anandpur Sahib in Punjab are colourful events that uphold their militant traditions.*

Page 119: *The Jain statue of Sravanabelagola in Karnataka rises 57 feet high, the world's largest monolith raised on a granite hill and approached by a steep, winding flight of rock cut steps. Erected in 983 AD, it dwarfs human visitors who toil up the steps to pay homage at the feet of this giant colossus.*

Opposite: *The Kandariya Mahadev temple at Khajuraho best embodies the excellence of the temple architecture for which the place has became known. Built over a period of a hundred years in the tenth and eleventh centuries by Chandela Rajput rulers, only 22 of the original 85 temples have survived, and in their facade follow a gradual uprise that replicates the high Himalayas.*

Above: *Erotica at Khajuraho. The sculptured temple tiers depict scenes from everday life, but it is for the sensuous carvings of erotica and woman in all her moods that these temples have become more known. It is presumed that these disturbing sculptures may have been carved on the temple walls to test the minds of the faithful.*

124

relief. While one interpretation has it that the sculptures were used to initiate young boys into the art of domestic living, another has it that their purpose was to test the faith of the believers, a third, more plausibe explanation is that the sculptures display a movement from the base to the spiritual, supported by the sculptures themselves which in the lower tiers deal with everyday life and end on the highest levels with images of gods and goddesses.

Khajuraho offers the visitor an unusual holiday for it is very much a small countryside retreat. You can hire a bicycle and explore the immediate environs, or take a taxi and visit a number of picturesque palaces, temples, water pools, forts, diamond mines and the Panna game sanctuary. An excursion to the palaces, forts and sumptuous halls of Orchha is rewarding, for this riverside town has charming fortified palaces and cenotaphs. Since Orchha falls halfway between Jhansi and Khajuraho, a trip can be planned to fit quite neatly into the itinerary.

Romantic citadels: Deeper into Madhya Pradesh in central India, 155 km from Indore is the scenic hilltop fort of Mandu, founded in the 10th century and perched on a 20 sq km plateau that drops steeply into a green valley with a river running through. While the setting itself is superb, Mandu, known euphemistically as the 'city of joy', is a grandiose township with buildings, palaces, subterranean pools, harems and tiered baths, all handsomely proportioned, and with enormous courtyards, tombs and a mosque patterned on that of Damascus, Syria.

Of the buildings on view, the unusual 'Ship Palace' or Jahaz Mahal is an imaginative structure built between two lakes to heighten the illusion of a floating ship. This was a royal harem, and a number of appointments, like a layered bath, add to its attraction.

Another whimsical structure is the 'Swing Palace' or Hindola Mahal, and a subterranean retreat near the lake shore which features a number of split-level pools, baths and water channels to ward off the summer heat. Hoshang Shah's Tomb is an exquisite mausoleum with a central dome surrounded by four smaller domes. It is believed that Shah Jahan sent his architects to study this tomb before drawing up plans for the Taj Mahal.

The romantic tale of Rupmati is tied in intrinsically with the green and marble citadel of Mandu. A beautiful Hindu singer, she was enticed by Emperor Baz Bahadur to come and stay at a beautiful pavilion constructed for her at the edge of the hillside which commanded a fascinating view. It is a gentle,

romantic structure which keeps the story alive for generations to come. Rupmati poisoned herself when the Mughals invaded Mandu.

Venturing south into the Deccan plateau, we experience a more even climate, a more languid pace and the southern answer to the Mughal splendours to be found in Delhi and Agra – the twin cities of Hyderabad and Secunderabad. This was the kingdom of the sumptuously rich and affluent Nizams of Hyderabad which was founded in 1590. A traditional city, located by the shore of the Musi river and the Hussain Sagar lake, Hyderabad retains its old world courtliness. The newer city of Secunderabad across Hussain Sagar is more modern and better laid out, on the lines of a British cantonment.

The most significant emblem that symbolises Hyderabad is the Charminar arch, built in 1591 to celebrate the end of the Hyderabad plague. The gateway is in the heart of a bustling bazar and has been immortalised on the yellow front of one of India's most popular cigarette brands. Next to the Charminar is one of the most impressive and largest mosques in the world. Made of granite, its construction began in 1614 and was finished in 1687. A Hindu shrine – the Birla Mandir – atop a rocky hill, is built entirely of white marble and offers an excellent view of the city.

Hyderabad's famous Salar Jung Museum contains 35,000 superb exhibits, collected from all over the world. Browsing through the rich array of jewelled swords, Persian miniatures, enormous paintings, ancient sculptures, voluptuous figures in stone and marble and unusual antiques, one loses track of time. The collection of a single individual, one of its most impressive pieces is the Italian marble statue called the Veiled Rebecca.

Pages 122-123: *The Indian countryside is crowded with monumental buildings, awesome forts, beautiful palaces, and temple spires such as these at Sainagiri close to Datia in the heart of the country.*

Opposite page, top: *The palace of Mysore, illuminated by night, highlights the architectural details of the residence of one of the most powerful ruling families of southern India. Today, Mysore has retained much of its stately charm, and continues to be known for its sandalwood and silk.*

Opposite page, bottom: *The Nandi Bull atop a Shiva temple in the Nandi Hills is a much revered and familiar statue, the mount of Lord Shiva.*

The Golconda Fort and the tombs of the Qutab Shahi kings are an interesting excursion into medieval India. Massive embattlements, huge gates, assembly halls, palaces and harems, and the great Durbar Hall with its superb acoustics, make a worthwhile sightseeing trip.

Deeper into the extreme south of Andhra Pradesh are two of India's most revered pilgrim places, definitely a must for any tourist who wishes to take a close look at Indian spiritual beliefs. Tirupathi and the holy hill of Tirumala are religious towns, devoted exclusively to pilgrim accommodation retreats. Amazingly neat and clean, the entire township is geared to feeding and sheltering a daily moving pilgrim strength of almost 5,000 devotees. The inner sanctum is open to non-Hindus and anyone is free to pray and ask for a wish in front of the image of Sri Balaji – a wish which Hindus implicitly believe to be granted when asked.

Southern splendour: Travelling into the adjoining state of Karnataka, formerly known as Mysore, the 11th-14th century Hoysala temples and ruins are worth the effort of a visit. Located primarily at Somnathpur, Belur and Halebid, the superb sculptures and detailed works of art to be found here rival the great works at Khajuraho and Konark. Another amazing ruined kingdom which is poignantly beautiful in its remains is Hampi, the capital of the Hindu kingdom of Vijaynagar of the early 1550s.

In Hampi's serene countryside, smooth contoured boulders are strewn amongst a hilly terrain. In this setting are the enormous ruins of what was once the capital of one of the largest empires in Indian history. It was a wealthy capital, since it controlled the rich spice trade, and was an international commerical centre. The ruins cover 33 sq km, the original city limits and the remains of seven concentric lines of fortification relating the story of another time and place in Indian history. One of the highest achievements of this period is an extremely fine rendering of sculpted work in the Vittala temple. Some of the works include an impressive stone chariot, and musical pillars. Other sites are the Lotus Palace, Dasara platform, Queen's bath and a watchtower.

The ruins of other, equally remarkably finished temples, their purity of content and execution, leave one moved at the impermanence of beauty and the relentless assault of time. Hampi today is a deserted township, miles from any modern city centre. The closest place is the small town of Hospet, and the nearest city is Bangalore, 358 km away.

Above: Southern palaces have a splendour at odds with the magnificence of their northern counterparts. The palaces of Mysore show minute attention to detail, including in the beautiful pillars.

Opposite page: Looking down from the monolithic statue of Sravanabelagola towards the township at the base of the hill on which the Jain figure stands in colossal majesty.

Hassan, a small township, is 119 km from the city of Mysore, and 70 km further are Belur and Halebid, 17 km apart. These remote villages are archaeological discoveries of what were once flourishing capital cities of powerful kingdoms. What is more, they represent a pinnacle of artistic development, rivalling the best in European Gothic art.

The Hoysaleswara Temple at Halebid was laboriously built and carved over a period of 80 years. What never ceases to amaze is the sheer detail of the project, as every centimetre of the exterior and interior wall is covered with exquisite carved panels, figures, intricate designs and stylised friezes depicting the life and times of the period. Carved out of soapstone which hardens with time, the medium proved best for the artistic expression of the time.

At Belur, the Channekeshava Temple is the only remaining structure of three Hoysala sites. Here, too, decorative art is at its exuberant best, and elaborate friezes smother outer and inner walls.

Mysore, which is 140 km from the state capital of Bangalore, is famous as the Sandalwood City of India, since it is situated in the heart of sandalwood country, where thick forests of rosewood, sandalwood and teak provide a rich source of commerce. As a result, some of the best handicrafts in these mediums can be found here. Inlay work and the famous Karnataka elephant in teak and rosewood are worthwhile souvenirs of this city, which is also the domestic centre of *agarbati*, or incense, for countrywide distribution.

Mysore is probably better known for its stunning Indo-Saracenic palace in the centre of the city which was the residence of the maharajas of Mysore, once a rich and powerful kingdom. This beautiful structure was rebuilt at colossal expense, after the original palace burned down. The structure is lavish with crystal, stained glass, mirrors, mosaic flooring, carved mahogany ceilings, immense silver doors and a profusion of gilt and bright colours as decorative touches.

Mysore has other palaces and handsome buildings too, and close by, on a hill that necessitates a healthy climb, is a statue of Nandi, Lord Shiva's mount, that is finely executed in a size that dwarfs visitors.

As an excursion base, Mysore is well suited for the ancient splendours of Hampi, Belur and Halebid. It is also a good base to see the fortress of Sirangapatnam built by Hyder Ali and Tipu Sultan, the superb temple carvings of Somnathpur, the ornamental Brindavan Gardens and fascinating wildlife sanctuaries – Bandipur, 80 km away; Nagarhole, 93 km away and the Ranganathittu bird sanctuary, 19 km away.

Bangalore is a beautifully planned city with a pleasant climate that lasts year round. The capital of Karnataka, Bangalore has long been known as a sophisticated, learned city though it is also a major industrial and commercial link of the south. It boasts busy shopping areas and fine textiles and silks, not to mention handicrafts and modern restaurants, hotels, parks, musical and cultural events. Of interest to the sightseer are the Lalbagh Botanical Gardens, laid in the 18th century and containing lotus ponds, a deer park and botanical treasures; Tipu Sultan's Summer Palace, the Bull Temple on Bugle Hill and Ulsoor Lake.

As a matter of interest, India's largest gold mines – the Kolar Gold Fields – are located 100 km east of Bangalore, and some of its shafts reach 3,000 metres under the ground.

Further into the Deccan plateau, about 351 km from Madras, towards the southern tip of the Indian peninsula, is Tanjore or Thanjavur, the ancient power centre of the dynamic Chola kings. It is interesting to know that under the Cholas, the southern kingdom became a great maritime power, in control of the sea routes across the Indian Ocean to China. The prosperous kingdom witnessed a

Opposite page: The structural temples of Belur and Halebid in Karnataka are full of sculptural details, buildings now in a wilderness that have an awesome, raw beauty. This sculpture of a goddess is from the facade of a wall in Belur.

Pages 130-131: Monks prostrate before the statue of Buddha at the Thai monastery in Bodh Gaya in Bihar. It was here that the Sakya prince gained Enlightenment and became the Buddha. The original Bodhi tree under which he had meditated still stands, having been replanted over the centuries as saplings from that original tree.

healthy patronising of the arts and we are able to see an outburst of creative energy both in Tanjore and in nearby regions. The city skyline is etched with temple spires and enormous *gopurams* of more than 70 religious shrines along with the battlements of a fort, observation towers and palace.

One of the most amazing examples of Chola architecture is the Brihadeshwara temple and fort. The temple itself has an 81 tonne dome carved out of a single piece of granite atop its 63 metre high temple roof. A massive Nandi bull guards the entrance to this thousand year old temple. Detailed frescoes and ornamentation cover the hard granite walls and are an indication of the sophistication in techniques used by artisans of that period.

The enormous palace complex is a vast, rambling structure, ruined in parts but grand nevertheless. It houses two fine museums with an excellent collection of stone and bronze statues of the 9th century and a fascinating collection of 30,000 palm-leaf and paper manuscripts. Tanjore is celebrated for metalwork repousse, bronze and inlay work in copper, brass and silver. Archaeology buffs can enjoy a series of temple constructions 40 km from Tanjore. Close to Tanjore is another famous temple town – Chidambaram – renowned for its great dancing Shiva figure, the famous Nataraja. This temple covers 13 hectares, and its towering 49 m high gouprams are closely covered with 108 classical postures of Shiva as Nataraja, the cosmic dancer. This excellent complex has a dance court with a thousand pillars across it, and one can only imagine the majesty and grace of dance programmes that were once held here.

Madurai, one of the principal cities of southern India, remains a great centre of Dravidian culture. Its focal point is the glorious Meenakshi temple which has nine *gopurams* or towers, each lavishly decorated with sculpted figures. The mind-boggling profusion of images explodes over every inch of available space. In front of the inner sanctuary is the 16th century hall of a thousand pillars with a stylised lion as motif.

A set of 'musical pillars', each of which strikes a different note and an attractive portico enclosing a water tank called the 'golden lotus' are worth viewing. The entire Meenakshi temple complex is a city within a city, and a climb to the top of the 45 metre *gopuram* is an unusual experience, since the stairs get gradually narrower and continue to wind endlessly till you reach the top, where you are rewarded with a magnificent view of Madurai and its environs – minus the soothing presence of a railing to hang onto.

The Buddha Trail

The influence of Buddhism on India is perceptible. From those many centuries ago when the Buddha walked the country to recent times have seen dramatic changes. In fact, at one stage Buddhism had all but vanished from India, though it flourished in neighbouring countries. Yet, today India is the seat of the exiled Tibetan spiritual leader, the Dalai Lama, a Nobel Prize laureate who is at the head of the international community of Buddhists. Buddhism is a palpable, living force with its roots in tranquillity, and with traditions and rituals that are rooted not only in the religion but in their lifestyle and living experiences.

In keeping with the spirit of the Buddha, most towns and cities connected with his life and times too reflect a restrained simplicity. One can begin the circuit from Lumbini (now in Nepal) at the foothills of the mighty Himalayas. This ancient hamlet was once a flourishing city in the kingdom of Kapilavastu, twenty five centuries ago. In 566 BC the birth of Siddhartha to a Sakya monarch began a story of unique dimensions. Siddhartha, later to become the Buddha or Enlightened One, spent his early years here. Very little remains except a small temple with the traditional seven metal plates featuring the Buddha and an Ashoka column which was built in 249 BC by Emperor Ashoka to mark this spot. A few monasteries provide a quiet retreat. There are plans to develop Lumbini into a major pilgrim spot by the Nepalese government.

One of the main Buddhist pilgrim spots connected with the Buddha is Bodh Gaya, close to Gaya in Bihar. In 531 BC the Buddha received enlightenment here, under the Maha Bodhi tree, which more than three thousand years later exists in its most venerated form today. Continually regenerated by its own saplings, the enormous tree with its many hanging roots has colourful buntings tied to it by ardent devotees.

Bodh Gaya is pilgrim city devoted solely to the Buddha and his teachings. The river Niranjana which flows nearby is also considered holy since the Buddha bathed here after receiving enlightenment. Close by is the sacred shrine of the Maha Bodhi temple with its dignified, ancient cast that reflects a great past. There is a magnificent sculpted figure of the Buddha in the earth-touching posture or 'Bhumisparsha Mudra' installed in the temple. Also of significance are casts of the Buddha's footprints in mortar which are heaped with floral offerings and sandalwood.

Nearby are several small shrines that pay homage to the spirit of the Buddha in touching ways : Ahimeshlochan Chaitya marks the place where the Buddha stood in gratitude after receiving enlightenment; Univilva on the banks of the Niranjana river is venerated since it is here that for six years the Buddha practised the severest austerities; Chankramana or jewelled walk is where the Buddha is believed to have paced up and down in deep thought.

In this quiet township, religious flags flutter in the breeze. The air hums to the sound of soft Buddhist hymns as robed monks serenely churn their prayer wheels. As a mark of respect, several monasteries and temples in distinct national styles have been constructed by the Burmese, Japanese, Chinese, Tibetans, Thai and Bhutanese — all countries that have been influenced by the teachings of the Buddha. Of particular interest is a Tibetan monastery which is dominated by a huge Dharma Chakra or Wheel of Law which must be rotated thrice to purify the worldly sinner. There is also an excellent museum which displays a varied collection of Buddha's bust and reclining figures in stone, bronze and even gold.

Rajgir, 65 km away, is a green, tranquil pilgrim spot dominated by a white marble temple built by the Japanese. This was once the capital of the powerful kingdom of Magadha. However, there are few tell-tale remains of this glorious period. We know that the first Buddhist Council was held in the existing Saptaparni caves immediately after the Buddha attained Mahaparinirvana. The sacred hill of Griddharkuta is associated with King Bimbisara's conversion to Buddhism. It was here that the Buddha delivered several sermons.

Nalanda is nearly as famous as Bodh Gaya. It was the intellectual nerve centre of Buddhism where over 10,000 students, monks and sages lived in monastic cells in the most prestigious university of the eastern world. The ruins of Nalanda are grand and evocative of its splendour in the 5th century AD. While the university itself was destroyed by Muslim marauders, and an invaluable library burnt, the vast brick remains of this spectacular university building evoke admiration and respect. One of the biggest monuments here is the Great Stupa flanked by flights of steps and terraces and a few votive stupas which are virtually intact.

A museum nearby has some interesting exhibits. Appropriately enough, a modern post graduate institute for international studies in Buddhism has been founded here.

One cannot bye pass Patna, the capital of the state of Bihar, although it is not connected with the Buddhist trail. Patna is the busy administrative centre of the state but was once an imperial city. While various Buddhist and Muslim monarchs did much to embellish the city, little remains of its past grandeur. There is the neo-classical Governor's Palace, the Patna Museum, the 90 ft bizarre Golghar – a granary, a whispering gallery, a heavily built mosque built in 1545, a venerated Sikh shrine and a vast building in Hazaribagh which once housed the East India Company's opium factory.

From Patna one may go north to Vaishali which was the 6th century BC capital of the Lichchavi empire – one of the first people to recognise the Buddha as a great philosopher. It must be remembered that the Lichchavis were probably the world's first people to adopt a republican form of government complete with an elected assembly of representatives.

The Buddha visited Vaishali several times and it was here that he preached his last sermon. To commemorate the last sermon, the Mauryan emperor, Ashoka, who was to become a devout follower, erected an 8.5 metre high lion pillar. This Ashokan pillar is made of polished red sandstone and the execution of the lions at the top of the pillar is detailed with such artistic skill that it has been made part of India's national emblem.

Another amazing stone structure is an 11.5 metre high column built by Ashoka in 249 BC on which six of the Buddha's edicts are inscribed.

Sarnath, 12 km from the sacred city of Varanasi, is a remote and tranquil spot where the famous Deer Park marks the spot where the Buddha preached his first sermon. It was here the Buddha first journeyed, following his enlightenment in search of his five disciples. Today, the area reveals many of the excavated sites of buildings belonging to the early years of Buddhist history. Sravasti, close to Lucknow, is another quiet township celebrated as the ancient capital of the Kosala kingdom where the Buddha confounded his critics with a miracle – a vision of a million self-manifestations seated on a thousand-petalled lotus.

At Kushinagar, 55 km from Gorakhpur, 10 ruined monasteries bear testimony to the importance of this site as the place where the Buddha passed into Mahaparinirvana. One can visit the Mukutabandhana stupa, said to have been built to preserve the Buddha's relics. A smaller, newer shrine now encloses a superb recumbent figure of the Buddha brought here by some tremendous feat by the monk Haribala between 413-455 AD all the way from Mathura.

Sanchi, in central India, 46 km from Bhopal, is the one place where superb examples of Buddhist creative art and sculpture can be seen. Here, one can clearly see the three basic tenets of Buddhist

architecture – the *Stupa* or monumental funeral mound; *Chaitya* or hall of worship; and the *Vihara* or monastery. The gateway of Sanchi is an instance of fabulous stonecraft. The reliefs depict the Jataka tales of the previous incarnations of the Buddha. Carved out of yellow stone and extremely well preserved, the four gateways detail chiselled images from the Buddha's life.

The Great Stupa itself is 106 ft in diameter and rises to a height of 42 ft. The Buddha's relics are said to be preserved here – well executed balustrades and umbrella forms atop the dome are exciting architectural features.

The Ajanta and Ellora caves, 40 km from Aurangabad, celebrate the Buddha's life and teachings. Here, in these world-famous caves, architects of yore constructed superb caves and then produced some of the finest existing paintings and sculptures known to man. Coloured in ochre, red, yellow and black, the Buddha's incarnations come to life. Drama, skill and technique flow into one another as entire walls are covered on a grand scale with depictions of the Jataka tales belonging to the first century BC.

Above: *The Dhamek Stupa at Sarnath, close to Varanasi, is an essential part of a Buddhist pilgrimage for it was here that the Buddha preached his first sermon in a deer park. The museum here also houses the Ashoka lion capital that is modern India's national emblem.*

Page 133: *At an initiation ceremony held at Sarnath and presided by the Dalai Lama, monks and novices from all over India gathered for the event.*

Journeys are forever. People come and go, and the eternal fascination of India endures. And when it's difficult to say goodbye, India has a popular saying that translates to mean 'I go, so I may return'.